We Have A Voice

We Have A Voice

LOUISE MOULTRIE

StoryTerrace

Text Aileen O'Brien, on behalf of StoryTerrace
Design StoryTerrace
Copyright © Louise Moultrie
Text is private and confidential

First print April 2021

StoryTerrace

www.StoryTerrace.com

CONTENTS

PROLOGUE — 9

FINDING MY VOICE — 13

1. EARLY DAYS — 21

2. RAGE — 29

3. TOO MUCH, TOO YOUNG — 37

4. PUBLIC PROPERTY — 45

5. ALONE — 53

6. HEAVEN AND HELL — 61

7. ESCAPE — 69

8. FALLING ON VELVET — 79

9. LOVE AND DESPAIR — 89

10. THE HEALING BEGINS — 101

11. RIGHTING WRONGS	113
12. NEW START	127
13. FACING THE STORM	139
14. THE JOURNEY CONTINUES	153
THANK YOU	165

For Derek and my sons

PROLOGUE

Two black children. I am one and the other is my brother. We are in a flat and I can see the busy London streets outside the bedroom window. We are wearing 70s clothes and I guess I am around eight, my brother slightly younger.

My mum, Fay, is screaming. There's a man beside her: tall, thin, softer. A safer adult. Fay pulls out a huge knife. She wants to hurt me, but I am standing up to her.

I am saying, "Just do it then." I am scared but I am not frightened of her anymore.

The man tells my brother to go into the other room to sleep, but then he follows him and I become both the children now, in both the rooms. This man, the safe person, starts to hold me down on the bed, he starts to kiss me and I can't move, the pressure of his body on me is a ton of weight.

I am thinking, *But I am a boy and you can't do this.*

His strength is almost superhuman and I am totally powerless, I cannot breathe or move. He is kissing my stomach and I am thinking, *Please, please help me! Stop, stop!* I am in total shock; my mind is so confused as he is meant to be the kind one, the father figure.

This monster weight is crushing me but my screams come

out as whispers. I am desperate for the people in the street below to save me, to hear me. My mum is in the next room through the open door. I am screaming with every bit of my exhausted energy, every part of my breath, so my sister can hear me.

"Help me! Please, please help me!"

It feels like an eternity. I have only dregs of breath left, it's like drowning, like someone holding your head under water and letting you up for a few seconds and putting you back under again.

This finally ends and my mum comes in the room, smiling. My sister, my alter ego, is listening to music on her headphones. She looks at me and I know she knows. It is a comfort but we both feel alone and scared and totally helpless. The lesson is: don't fight the adult, don't think you have a voice, don't go up against Fay. None of the children is safe and no one will help us.

The dream switches swiftly from horror film to a well-lit, happy scene. A girl's bedroom. I am the girl now, sitting on a bed with another girl, my friend. We are connected by the same headphones. I have a reel-to-reel cassette player and I am planning to record a message to tell someone I am in danger and get them to rescue me. I know I have to be careful and my friend is my cover, we look like we are playing. My plan is to escape my mum. She is outside my bedroom door, which I have shut with a bolt on my side. Then I realise that the bolt is actually on her side. She slides it across and pushes open the door. Now she is watching us.

"She is up to no good," says Fay to the man beside her. "She's up to something."

I wake up. I am in my bed in 2020 and I am in my home. My body is shaking and I am hyperventilating, woken from my dream by my gasps for breath and strangled cries. I spend the next 20 minutes with my husband, Derek, who holds my hand and rubs my arms.

"I am here Lou," he says softly. "It's a dream, darling. You're OK."

I sob so loudly, like never before. I'm still catching my breath and I feel my heart is being kickstarted, as if I have been pulled from a lake and my body revived at the side of the road by paramedics.

The ambulance is here. The ambulance is Derek's arms, holding me. I am safe and he is strong. I sob and sob. I know it's a dream. I was both those children: being a black child resonates with not being heard. I know, with all my wondrous new insight, that I need to feel how safe I am in the here and now, and I need to ground myself.

I get up, still shaking, tears rolling down my face, but I know I am OK. I walk into my kitchen and make myself a cup of tea. I look around my lovely home and light my candles. It's 5 a.m. and still dark outside. I open my front door, feel the cold on my face and I take a deep breath of fresh air. I look out to the road and see the shop light turn on, the guy pulling the papers in. I hear Derek in the bedroom. I have wrapped myself in my soft dressing gown and as I sit in my front room in my safe, beautiful home, I know what the dream was saying: that the me who was the child did escape. I am safe, I am home and I made it to adulthood.

I have love and I have a voice. I can tell my story and this book is it.

FINDING MY VOICE

That was a dream I had the night before I started working on this book. And so I begin. This is me, this is my story of abuse in the home and how the trauma has impacted my young and adult life. It may not always be easy reading but I believe that, in the end, it is a story about healing and hope.

I am currently fighting the most intense and horrendous part of my recovery from the many years of sexual and violent abuse I suffered in my childhood. For many years I could not look at, or even acknowledge those buried memories, choosing instead to soothe myself with food and alcohol, among other things. When I could no longer ignore my trauma and began to feel its full effect, I wanted to take my own life. This was not a cry for help or a dramatic ending to a shitty past, but an attempt to relieve the utter ball-breaking distress I experienced every day.

However, I have made it! I am now 50 years old and have everything to live for. I have a warm, beautiful and safe home to go to every night. Yes, I have been very happily married for the last 30 years to the most amazing man, with whom I have two wonderful sons. In my mind they will always be my beautiful babies (they will cringe at this of course!), but they are now fully-grown men in their late 20s and I could not be prouder of them both. The fact I had a hand in creating and rearing them brings me such joy and hopefulness for other individuals out there. I also have my grandson who warms my heart. I am now only connected to family members I trust and love. I have a couple of very special friends, not great numbers, but enough for me. I truly love this part of my life.

This is the part of me that wants very much to be alive forever, to be around to laugh, love and to see my kids and their kids get old. To see my cousins crack jokes and reminisce, as families do, about funny things.

On the other side, there is a part of me that can take over suddenly when I'm relaxing in my home, talking to my sons, or at work. This is the part of me that starts to shrink from the confident and bubbly person who loves life. I become the small, lonely, terrified child who has no one to talk to and feels completely unloved and alone. This is where everything goes dark. The world begins to feel heavy, unsafe, unwelcoming and I am back in the intense misery that once plagued my life. I feel that I am no longer that person who has everything to live for, the nice home, the caring husband, the brilliant sons. This is trauma. I have come a long way in my recovery but the trauma never goes away completely.

For many years, when I experienced these bouts of negative thoughts, I would ease my distress with overeating and binge drinking, in my younger years through smoking (not just tobacco), shoplifting and sniffing glue. I was reckless with sex and in my 20s carried a police cosh and snooker balls should anyone attack me. I must stress that I have never condoned or participated in violence, but after years of being the recipient of beatings and verbal rages from my own mother, and sexual violence (forced oral rapes) committed by my step-grandfather, I felt the world was an unsafe place. I think now, some 30 years later, I would have been diagnosed with complex PTSD at the very least. I was like a traumatised soldier, always ready for an attack.

For a long time, alcohol gave me the numbness and distraction I craved. When I was drunk I could laugh, dance and socialise, have sex and no feelings, never connecting with my anxious and vulnerable self. The noise of a party can drown out anything. Overeat Sunday to Thursday, then drink Friday and Saturday and you can avoid all those scary feelings.

Eventually, there came a time for the real healing to begin. Alcohol could no longer be the crutch and fake friend it had been for so much of my life. With the help of therapy, training, books and talking, I have managed to overcome most of my self-harming addictive behaviours, swapping them for a healthier, happier version of myself. Through years of therapy I was able to process my traumas, put the pieces of the puzzle together and realise that I wasn't mad.

I was having a completely understandable reaction to a terrible trauma perpetrated by the people I should have been able to trust most in the world. My behaviour was a consequence of years of abuse and I had developed ways to block it out, hide and delete all the memories. Ah, but they don't go anywhere. They just sit in a part of your brain, waiting to surface.

I struggle to remember a lot of my story. Up to the age of 19, it comes to me in fragments, which is your first lesson in my trauma. My abuse disturbed the way my brain recalls my life. I was unable to process day-to-day life because I was too traumatised. So I coped by shutting it all out. But the trauma was still there, biding its time.

I was finally able to get rid of booze, food and most other negative coping mechanisms, but that means I now have to sit with all the feelings and memories that the food and booze had blocked out. Now I have the unenviable task of letting my emotions surface. And when I struggle to cope, I let people know instead of drinking those feelings down. It's weird, I feel far more vulnerable now than I ever did, but I also know I am far healthier than I ever believed possible.

I doubt I will ever report my mum's abuse. It would never help me or my family and I feel it would cause me great emotional pain. Instead, I use all I know to support and educate women and children. My work for the past 20 years has been all about supporting those affected by sexual and domestic abuse. It's all I want to do and it helps me feel less helpless and powerless while women and children continue to suffer.

I want nothing more from life than to be calm, happy and safe. This book is not about the perpetrators. They will continue to live in denial. It's about me and my survival through the abuse, the impact it has had and the rollercoaster journey that women like me never speak about. It's about wanting my sons to never ever be quiet about what's wrong in the world and it's about them knowing it's OK to not be OK sometimes.

I am dedicating the book to my awesome husband but I am writing it for my boys. I want them to understand what happened to me and how that affected me and my behaviour. I wasn't born traumatised. I was exposed to trauma by adults who failed and abused me. I want my sons to know they are the reason I have fought so hard to be alive and be happy, but also how hard that has been sometimes.

A gentle word of advice: before you start reading this book, whether you are a family member, work colleague, survivor or victim of abuse, woman, man, friend or foe, it is important to take care of yourself. After each chapter, or even page, just check out how you are feeling in your mind and in your body. It's all connected, it's a valuable part of self-care to acknowledge your responses. If you feel disconnected, wobbly, angry, upset, or hurt, take time out if you need to. It's just a book and I am just a person. It's you that is important, so do whatever you need to look after yourself. Validate what you feel and come back to it when it's good for you. Some of us will be triggered or connect deeply with things I have written about, so self kindness is the only way forward.

I am, of course, hoping you will enjoy the read. That would be a real plus. I hope you will get to know me better and maybe get to know yourself better, understand my life and learn about people. This book is not just about my voice, it's about everyone who has suffered at the hands of another. It is about challenges I have faced and things you may also face and it is about recovery. It's about not changing historical trauma but understanding its complexities. Thank you for taking the time to read my story. Let's start!

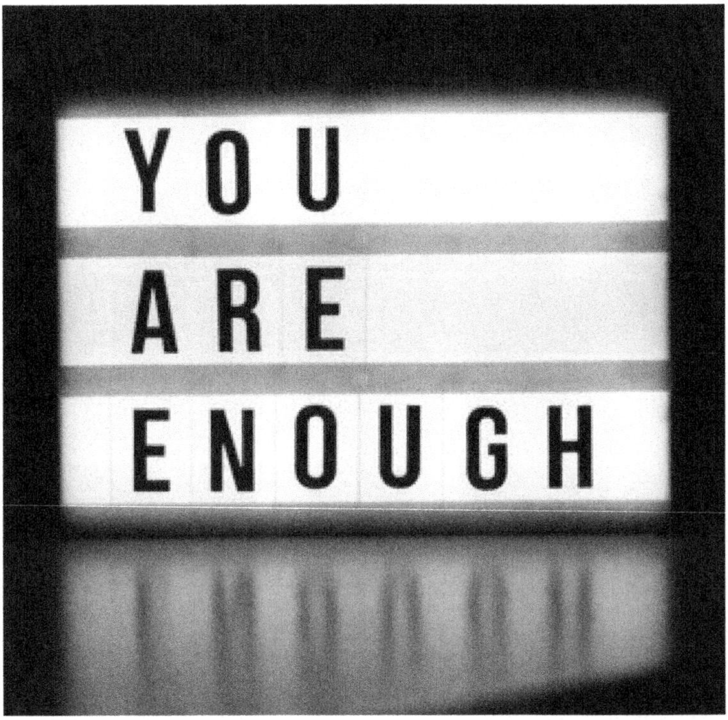
YOU
ARE
ENOUGH

1
EARLY DAYS

Soundtrack: Desmond Dekker - 'The Israelites', Janis Joplin, Staple Singers - 'Respect Yourself', Bill Withers, Motown

Music has always been massively important to me: it is my escape, my comfort, my joy, my constant companion. Some songs transport me immediately to a certain time and place, and for every period of my life I have an unforgettable playlist. I couldn't tell my story without including the soundtrack that colours all my memories.

I am standing in my cot and I can hear my mum screaming and shouting. There's someone there, a man I think. I feel frightened and distressed.

This is my first memory of my mum, Fay, and it's quite blurry. We were living in a bedsit at the time. I was a toddler and Fay was a very young single mother. She was just 15 when I was born in Croydon hospital in February 1969. I was quite a cultural mix: Anglo-Burmese on my mum's side and Anglo-Indian on my dad's. Gordon, my dad, was 21 when I arrived, not yet ready to settle down, so my mum had me on her own.

This was a time when young single mums were being forced to give up their children for adoption, so it can't have been an easy time for her. I remember my mum screaming and shouting a lot. I have an image from when I was a two-year-old of her standing at the door raging at my dad, who must have come to see me. Sometimes I would wake up and there would be strange men in the flat, sitting with my mum on the settee. There were always records being played: Desmond Dekker's 'The Israelites' was on all the time, along with Janis Joplin. I loved music. I guess my mum, as a teenager living independently for the first time, was doing her best to have fun.

She had a job in a bar at one point. I don't know what she did with me, but I learned later that one of her neighbours complained about her leaving me alone so often. She hadn't started being violent to me yet. I have a sense of me being physically close to Fay, of her carrying me around. I would never be so close to her again. I loved my mum but I always felt scared around her as a child.

When I was about four, she met my stepdad, George, and I have an image of being shut outside their room when they were in bed. I would stand outside the closed door, screaming and crying to be let in. This was how family life would play out for the rest of my childhood and beyond –

me on the outside, not allowed in. Even before I became my mother's punchbag, I had an overwhelming sense of loneliness in those early years with her.

It wasn't like that at my nan's house. I loved going to stay with my nan, Fay's mum, at weekends. Me and Nan would spend hours together, talking, going shopping and cooking. She would do lovely things like cut up my sandwiches into quarters and hold my hand when we went out anywhere. I loved my nan. But although I felt warm and cared for at her house, something wasn't right. The secret was locked inside me, a dark, very early memory lurking around the edges of my mind, trapped inside my body. It remained buried for a long time, appearing to me now and then as a flashback. It was over 40 years later, with the help of a trauma therapist, that I was unable to unlock this preverbal memory. How do you have words to describe the unimaginable?

My nan's second husband, Tony, was a sexual predator who violated me in my cot when I was barely a year old and carried on abusing me for over a decade.

Tony was about 25 years younger than my nan and she adored him. He was a friend of Nan's sons, my uncles Derrick and Warren, who were also abusive. It turned out that abuse ran through generations of my mum's family.

My nan didn't really like to talk about her past. I asked her once about the scars on her legs and why her toenails were so badly deformed. She told me it was because of the trek she'd done through the jungle to flee from Burma after the war. Thousands began the trek and only 300 people survived. Nan described how she would wake up in the swamp, leeches on her body, corpses all around her. It was a rare glimpse into her early life, which she would tell me about every now and then.

She had a very English-sounding name, Molly Florence Smith, but her mother was Burmese and her father, a railway worker, was Irish. She grew up in Burma, one of the youngest among 12 or so children. Her family was wealthy and privately educated, which is probably why my nan spoke such perfect English, like the Queen. Her siblings were doctors, lawyers and teachers and my nan was a nursing sister. She married Hugh, who was quite high up in the army and they had four children – three boys and my mum, Fay. Nan told me that her husband Hugh used to hurt her. She didn't go into too much detail but she said he was an angry man who would sometimes rip off her clothes in front of the crying children. So there was already exposure to violent abuse and, I am absolutely sure, rape.

They were living in Singapore at this point but, eventually, Nan decided to move to England because her oldest son, Derrick, got into gangs and knife crime. So they moved to Croydon. Her husband, Hugh, was supposed to follow on and bring money but he gambled it all away and didn't come. So Nan was on her own with no money and four children in a strange country. She wasn't even able to work as a nurse because her qualifications weren't recognised over here.

Then along came Tony. Nan would have met Tony in Singapore when he was friends with her sons and then he also moved to England. I don't know whether he came over at the same time as Nan or later, but he also settled in Croydon. Nan must have been drawn to him, not least because he was nothing like Hugh. Tony was kind and good fun, the life and soul of any party, the sort of man that everyone liked…

When I was three I went to Munich with Nan and Tony to attend my Uncle Derrick's wedding. I don't recall what happened exactly but I do remember feeling an intense fear at nighttime. I know Tony did something to me on that trip. My body remembered it, even if my mind didn't.

Trauma does not lie, even though perpetrators may try to say that it does. So-called 'false memory syndrome' is brought up by perpetrators to try and discredit a victim and make her out to be a liar. It's shocking that women who have been raped may have to wait until two years after their court case for therapy, simply so no one can claim that the therapy has brought out a false memory. The body does not lie, the body remembers. I couldn't recall what happened in Munich but I remember the physical terror, my body shaking with fear. I could not remember the horror that occurred in my cot when I was barely a year old, but whenever I had flashbacks to it, my face and jaw would freeze and lock as a physical memory of oral abuse.

My first conscious and clear memory of Tony as a sexual

perpetrator was when I was about three or four years old. I suffered badly from asthma and my nan would rub Vicks (menthol balm) on my chest and back to help me breathe. One night, I was lying in the front room with the telly on and my eyes closed, pretending to be asleep. Someone had come into the room, it must have been my nan, I thought, because there was that comforting smell of Vicks, which she was rubbing on my chest. Then I heard a man's cough, it was not my nan but Tony. I didn't think anything of it until he put his hand into my knickers and started touching me. I didn't understand, I didn't like it and I knew this was somehow not right. I wondered where my nan was. Then I heard my uncle in the hall, saying he was off. He was standing just outside the door. That's how brazen Tony was. He helped himself to my body right under everyone's noses.

I spent a lot of time at my nan's house with her and Tony. I liked being there because it was calm and peaceful and I felt loved. It was always better than the alternative. Strange as it may sound, I didn't feel unsafe there like I did at home. I don't really remember a time with my mum when I felt safe and loved. And once Fay's rages began, being at home was a living hell.

2
RAGE

Soundtrack: *Tina Charles, Gary Glitter, Bay City Rollers, Elvis, Boney M, David Soul*

Fay is shouting in my face and hitting me. As her furious punches rain down on my body, I melt away in my head. I block out the stinging slaps, the rageful screams. I am not here, I feel no pain. But there is someone sobbing. I realise it's me. I hate her with all my heart.

Fay's vicious beatings could happen at any time and for any reason. She would find a reason to blame and shame me and there was no one to stop her assaults. My survival instinct taught me to become numb, to zone out from her anger, her rage and her disgust at me for whatever it was this time. It didn't matter what had caused Fay to give me a beating, I had stopped looking for any reason or justice. As far as my mum was concerned I was always in the wrong and always to blame. I deserved this.

I now had a half brother, Jeff, who was six years younger than me, plus a stepbrother and sister from George's first marriage. Delaine and Jim lived with their mum, but at weekends they would often come to stay with us at our flat on Duppas Hill Road in Croydon. I remember Jim came to live with us for a while.

We lived in that flat from the mid to late-1970s and it was a very stressful, unhappy time for me. Most of my memories are filled with Fay's fury. I remember watching her having fights at bus stops, arguing in shops, being aggressive in queues, always aggressive, always fighting. I was with her one time when she stole meat from a shop, she didn't shield me from anything. There was no peace, home was not a safe place. Even dinner time was stressful because Fay would scream at me to eat up everything, to not be wasteful. Not surprisingly, I developed an unhealthy relationship with food. From the age of six, I would comfort eat and began a cycle of overeating, bingeing and being sick that would last well into my adult life.

I have many miserable memories in that flat. When I was around seven, my mum lost a pair of nail scissors. I had my own pair and when Mum saw me with them, she accused me of stealing hers.

"You fucking had them!" she screamed.

Needless to say, she gave me a good beating, despite my protests that the scissors were mine. When she eventually found her own scissors, there was no apology – and never would be.

Nothing was done with love. From cleaning my ears with a metal hairpin, to yanking my hair when she brushed it, there was always pain and punishment. I was a very unhappy little girl and many a night I had nightmares that would make me cry in my sleep. And I was so lonely. Sometimes I escaped reality by creating an imaginary world with my dolls and making tents from blankets out on our balcony.

If home was full of misery, school was a wonderful relief. I loved school. I felt safe there and looked after, even the little bottles of milk that we had at break made me feel nurtured. I didn't tell any of my teachers about what was going on at home, but the signs were there. One day I was looking so upset that a teacher asked me what was wrong. I told her that my mother was going to cut off all my hair that night and I didn't want her to. The teacher tried to reassure me that my mum would never do such a thing, but she didn't know my mum. Fay had promised me that she was cutting off my hair because I had tangles in it, I couldn't brush it properly. I had begged her not to, but I knew she would. True to her word, Fay hacked off all my hair and it was so butchered that when I went to school the next day, I wore a hood. My teacher asked me to take off my coat and when I wouldn't she pulled off my hood. And in that moment, the teacher knew. But no words were spoken about it. Thankfully, safeguarding in schools means children are much better protected now. But

I was left to feel ugly and helpless. I knew that the teacher couldn't help me. No one could help me.

It's difficult now to even put into words the far-reaching, deep impact made by this incident. It was such an angry, violent act, such a terrible thing to do to a little girl. I will never forget how scared I was when she did it, nor the sheer despair I felt at losing my precious hair. It's unthinkable that a mother would do that to her own child. It was savage and downright cruel, one of the many cruel things Fay did that damaged my self-belief and that still trigger me today. I remember, years later, watching Mommie Dearest, a biographical film that depicted actress Joan Crawford as an abusive, manipulative mother who hurt her adopted children. There was a scene in which Joan cuts off her daughter's hair and I watched it in horror. I identified with this little girl on every level. It made me sob and sob. Decades later, Fay's cruelty was still traumatising me.

After this brutal haircut, I realised how unsafe I was, how alone and powerless. She owned me, all of me, even my hair, and she had shown me that she could do what she wanted with me. She was destroying who I was and made me feel I was nothing, a transparent shell. I coped with the hurt by pushing it down deep inside me and carrying on as though nothing was wrong.

It was only years later that I heard the word dissociation. It's something that most survivors of terror experience and it's how the brain protects us from trauma. When you dissociate you block out memories and disconnect from emotions. That's how I coped all through my childhood and well into adulthood. I was so good at burying my internal distress that I appeared to be a happy young girl living a perfectly happy life.

I wasn't the only person in my mum's family to be suffering in silence. Fay's brothers, Derrick and Warren, were charismatic and attractive, just like my mum. I remember going to family parties and here were these outwardly charming, generous, well-dressed uncles. But they were violent abusers, just like my mum. Behind closed doors they beat their wives, cheated on them and scared their children. My mum also told me that they had beaten her in their family home and that my nan had done nothing to stop it.

Even as a child I could feel the fear when I went to my uncles' houses. Their wives, beaten into submission, were terrified of them. Yet no one ever challenged these rage-filled bullies. Derrick and Warren, along with my mum, were no doubt damaged by their own trauma as children. The rage was in them all, except for the youngest brother, Chris. He seemed to have escaped the worst of the trauma, perhaps because he came over to England when he was very young and wasn't brought up by his abusive dad. Chris was calm and soft, a loving parent and to me he was a bubbly uncle, always laughing. I laugh myself now to think what great delight he took in winding up his Tory-voting siblings by telling them he was supporting the Green Party. I will always remember being in a van with Chris and his wife as they talked about how they should give up smoking for the sake of their children. I thought this was wonderful: a parent putting their children before themselves. What, I wondered, would that be like?

It was my dad's side who gave me some loving memories of family life. I looked forward to going to my dad's because it felt so different, it was so calm. I loved my dad and I loved my stepmum, Frances, an amazingly compassionate, warm woman with a beautiful Irish accent, who always looked so pleased to see me. I have good memories of gentle, kindly family members from Dad's side. When I picture my time with them, I think of laughing, watching cartoons with my cousins, playing Scrabble, food, music, cuddles and happiness. Love, in other words, normal family love.

That's also what I enjoyed when I went to visit my nan's brother-in-law and his wife. Mervyn and Rita were my godparents and they were wonderful. They had about eight kids and I used to really enjoy going to stay with them in Huntingdon. The house was chaotic and messy, always full of kids, of people letting themselves in through the back door. It was all softness, fun and watching telly perched on the arms of chairs, surrounded by my lovely second cousins. It was totally unlike family life in Croydon, more like The Royle Family. When she was there with me, Fay rarely showed her rages. Maybe being surrounded by love had a good effect on her, too. But the magic spell ended once we returned home.

There were often people staying at our house, including Fay's brother Warren and one of George's friends at different times. Fay was always taking people in and showing them her caring side. Once again, there were similarities to Mommie Dearest: a mother taking in orphans and being charitable to others, yet cruel and controlling to her own children.

Meanwhile, at my nan's house, the sexual abuse continued. Tony didn't let anything stop him, he had the power to abuse me when there were other people around. There were times he violated me right under my nan's nose, as I slept next to them on the floor on a put-you-up bed. I would have my eyes tightly shut and held my breath as he put his hands under the blankets, touching me. He was always touching me, his hand between my legs or on my chest, and tickling me in front of other people. To this day if anyone tries to tickle me, I am triggered and my body reacts before my brain can process that I am safe, sending me instantly into fight mode. That's the trauma in my body.

Despite Tony, I still loved going to my nan's because it was a peaceful refuge away from Fay's unrestrained rages. I would spend whole summers there and I have lovely memories of going on trips with Nan and my cousin Troy. She was gentle, caring, affectionate – everything my mum was not. Nan showed me the love my mum seemed incapable of giving. She never shouted at me, or hit me, she never dragged me around, never told me I was stupid. I always wanted to go and stay at her house, despite the sexual predator living there – that's a measure of how miserable I was at home. If my mum hadn't been so aggressive, I know everything would have been very different. I would have felt safe to have spoken out about Tony. But as it was, I pushed everything down and stayed silent.

3

TOO MUCH, TOO YOUNG

Soundtrack: Streetband – 'Toast', 10cc – 'Dreadlock Holiday', Eagles, The Commodores – 'Three Times a Lady', Grease soundtrack, Abba, Wings – 'Mull of Kintyre', Stevie Wonder – 'Ebony and Ivory', Northern Soul, Bob Marley – 'Redemption Song', Pink Floyd – 'Another Brick in the Wall'

"Fuck off! Just get on your bike and fuck off!" My mum's face is contorted and ugly as she screams at me. "I'm sorry," I plead. "I didn't mean it." Her frenzied shouting seems to go on for an eternity. The fear is making me numb, I cannot focus and my brain is starting to shut down. Then everything comes into sharp focus again as she opens the door and pushes me outside before chucking my bike down the stairs. "And don't fucking come back! I don't want to see you again."

What had I done to provoke this torrent of abuse? I had asked my mum if I could go outside to play. I was nine years old and it was such a lovely, sunny day that I was keen to go out and ride my bike. In my eagerness I made the mistake of asking her twice.

That was it. Fay flew into one of her unbridled rages that sent me spinning into a spiral of frozen distress and tearful apology. After she had slammed the door shut, I stood sobbing on the stairs, confused and desperate. I couldn't think straight and didn't know what to do. My mum had said she didn't want me and that I shouldn't come back. I believed her. I struggled down two flights of stairs with my heavy bike and rode around aimlessly for what seemed like hours, through subways and the old town and then to Waddon where a schoolfriend lived.

I knocked on her door and asked my friend if I could come in because my mum told me I couldn't go home. I was sobbing. My friend's mum came to the door and said her little girl had to go now, closing the door. I got it: they did not want to get involved with this disturbed child. This wouldn't be the only time during my childhood when I would go to someone else's house, crying and distressed, seeking support.

After my friend's mum shut the door on me, I rode around, distraught, until I found myself outside some shops not too far from our flat. My mum's half sister walked past and said hello but I didn't speak to her. I didn't know what to say. I realise now I was in shock. I went to the red phone box and used the 2p in my pocket to call my nan. The next thing I remember is being at the door of our flat with an adult beside me, either Nan or Tony. Mum was at the door, yelling at me. She was angry that I had called my nan and she was angry that I had been rude to her sister by ignoring her. I don't recall the details of being allowed back into the flat but I know there was no apology. In Fay's mind there was no need, it was all my fault.

I know now that my mum is not well. She is a very damaged individual, no doubt with a personality disorder. I realise she is too ill and too disturbed to ever accept responsibility for any of her actions. Whatever abuse she suffered is her story to tell, but instead of processing her own trauma, she projected all the hate she had for herself onto me. This is what I know as an adult, with all my knowledge and experience. Now that I have my own children and know that I would do anything on earth to protect my boys and to save them from a second of sadness or pain, my mother's behaviour seems all the more horrific.

But when I was a little girl of nine, I didn't understand any of this. I felt that it was all my fault. My mum blamed me for all the upset surrounding the bike incident and I knew she was right, I had caused it all. No wonder my mother didn't want me, I was a horrible, unlovable child. I was left feeling exhausted, empty and totally unloved – and all because I had asked my mum if I could play on my bike.

I was always on the outside of our family. It seemed to me that I had my nose pressed to the window, looking in. While I got on well with my stepbrother and sister, I wasn't at all close to my stepdad George during those early years. He never did anything to protect me from my mum and never did anything that made me feel included in his family. Fay would often put me to bed earlier than my siblings, even though I was the oldest. So I would go off to bed, leaving Jeff, Delaine and Jim cuddling their dad. I would often see Fay kneeling by his side, she was besotted with him. When he came home from work Fay would take off his boots for him, the very picture of love. Seeing this tenderness between them, a tenderness that I never received, made me feel all the more excluded.

My mum treated me like a slave rather than a daughter. From a very young age I had to do all the chores around the house and woe betide me if Fay spotted anything not done perfectly. George would send me out to the shops over and over again until I thought I was going mad. To them, I was an object to be used, not a person.

Though I think she did sometimes hit my younger brother Jeff, Fay saved most of her violence for me. It was as though my mere existence irritated her. She seemed to delight in humiliating me in front of visitors, friends, workmates and family. I remember her ripping off my blouse just before I was about to perform at a school event, hitting me around the face at a children's party, being so horrible and screaming at me so badly at a family wedding that my nan and Uncle Chris had to intervene. George was never at these events, he never came anywhere with us as a family until we were adults.

I was so unhappy at home that being in hospital was a welcome relief. I was quite a bad asthmatic as a child and was admitted many times onto the children's wards at Croydon's Mayday hospital. The peace and quiet was so beautiful. I didn't care that I couldn't breathe, being treated kindly was like a breath of fresh air to me. It was so soothing to be away from my mother, in a place where adults actually smiled at me. Being cared for felt so special and so foreign to me.

There was no end to Fay's cruelty. One day she chucked my radio out of the window in one of her rages. My dad had bought me that radio and I loved it. Listening to songs was my escape, my happiness, my time to forget. It was also a connection to my dad, who shared my love of music. Fay knew how much it meant to me, so what better way to punish me than to destroy it? She was relentless in chasing out anything that was good in my life. Yet, despite everything, I still yearned for her love. I wanted her to cuddle me and stroke my face, to be gentle. I wanted her to say, even once, that I was pretty, that she was sorry, that she didn't mean it. I longed for her to give me comfort, anything at all, so that I could feel special and lovable for even the briefest moment.

I found my comfort in music. For a good few years I spent every break and lunchtime at school singing in the playground, mostly Abba songs from their Waterloo album. I learned all the words and sang my heart out. If it wasn't Abba it was Elvis. Often I would sing Abba songs with my friend Antonia – she was the dark one and I was the blonde

– or I would sing on my own. I didn't care who was looking or what they thought, I was lost in music in the playground and it was magical.

Round at my nan's house there was often music playing on the stereo because they had a lot of parties. One party in particular stands out. It must have been during the 70s because I remember big hair, flares and flowery shirts. The house was heaving with family members, but this wasn't going to stop Tony from getting what he wanted. My older cousin Troy and I had gone to bed and we were pretending to be asleep under the blankets when Tony came in. He tried to pull the cover off me and abuse me while Troy lay in the bed next to me. But when Troy and I started laughing, Tony told us to go to sleep and he left. When Troy asked what Tony was doing, I told him Tony came into the bedroom all the time.

"Shut up, don't be stupid!" said Troy in disbelief. Nothing more was said.

Then, later on, I got up to go to the loo and Tony pulled me into the bathroom. I couldn't pretend to be asleep anymore. He tried to kiss me and put his tongue in my mouth. I tasted peanuts on his tongue, which made me feel even more sick because I was allergic to them. When I started screaming for Tony to stop, he put his hand on my mouth. Troy started banging on the bathroom and toilet doors, wondering where I was. When I was back in bed, Troy asked me where I'd been and I told him I was in the bathroom.

Troy said, "No, you can't have been in there because I saw Tony coming out." He just didn't get it.

Tony was so prolific in his abuse of me that I became sexualised. There was one point, at the age of about eight or nine, when I enjoyed his attention. I remember being on the couch with me on top of him, cuddling up to him and thinking, Oh, can we feel like that now because it feels nice. And other times I would roll down my knickers, ready for him. This is the complicated truth of abuse.

The fact that I had been conditioned to expect it, and that my body responded to it, doesn't diminish the crime or its depravity, it just shows how the perpetrators manipulate their victims. Paedophiles prey on the vulnerable, children like me, starved of love and attention at home and with no adult protection. A child's body can respond to touch and both a girl and boy can orgasm, even in fear. This is not a sign of enjoyment, this is a normal response to stimulation. Paedophiles know this, children don't and they often feel shame or feel to blame for what the perpetrator has done. It is never the child's fault.

Most of the time I didn't enjoy Tony's attention and as time went on I hated it. I tried to protect myself from it as best I could but I was fighting a losing battle. I knew I was never safe, not even with family around. Except for one night. This night, at my nan's, I was sharing a double bed with Mervyn and Rita's daughters, Geraldine and Debbie, who I loved and trusted. Knowing what Tony was capable of, I asked them if I could sleep in the middle, in between them, so I slept flanked by my lovely second cousins. That was one night he couldn't get to me.

4

PUBLIC PROPERTY

Soundtrack: *Madness – 'The Prince', Squeeze – 'Up the Junction', Dire Straits – 'Romeo and Juliet', UB40 – 'Present Arms', Frankie Miller – 'Darlin''. Tony's record collection: Don Williams, Charlie Pride, Tammy Wynette, Elvis, Loretta Lynne, The Furys, John Denver, Nana Mouskouri, Dolly Parton, Top of the Pops albums of the 60s and 70s. The Specials, The Beat*

I wake up and he is there, standing over me, lying next to me. Him and his fucking hands. He's trying to kiss me: my mouth, my neck, my under-developed breasts, my down below, my everything. Yes my bloody body, my shitty body, my disgusting piece of meat body. How did he get in? The fucking useless lock on the door. I never hear him come in. I am wrapped up tight in my bedding, a human sausage roll. He is now a magician, he's unwrapped my mummified body while I slept and he is aroused. He tries to force his erect penis into my tightly shut lips, into my hand; this hard, awful skin-thing trying to push its way into me. I am choking, I am going to be sick, I am going to die.

When I was 10 I spent a lot of time at my nan's. I started sleeping in her back room and, at last, had a lock on my bedroom door. The idea of having any boundaries, any privacy, was such a novelty. I didn't even have a door on my bedroom at home. It was only a small lock, a little bolt that you could slide across, but I knew it would make a huge difference to me. I could keep Tony out.

Whenever I stayed at Nan's, I would test it out, sliding the bolt across and back until I was satisfied it worked. Then, at bedtime, I would hammer it shut with my shoe – there was no way he was getting in. Just to make myself even safer, I would roll myself up tightly in my sheet and quilt. It was so hot in there that I went to sleep barely able to breathe. I didn't care – if I could have vacuum-packed myself in my bedding I would have. I wanted to send a clear message: I was not to be unwrapped, touched, licked, kissed, fingered, penetrated. But it was all useless. I would wake up and there he was, next to me.

I never heard him coming. How had he got in? I still don't know to this day, but he was a child abuser, he would always find a way. I sometimes played dead, thinking he would give up if I was unresponsive. But it didn't stop him, he didn't give a shit if I was conscious or not. He would hold my limp hand on top of his dick, moving my hand faster and faster as I lay there inert.

It was my fault, I was so stupid. I hadn't locked the door carefully enough, I hadn't wrapped myself up tightly enough. I hated that room and the one next to it and every room in that house because he had abused me in all of them.

Whenever I hear Frankie Miller's 'Darlin'' it makes me think of those disgusting times with Tony. To me, it was a house of horror, but to the outside world it was a welcoming, sociable place where Tony was the genial host at their many parties. He knew how to make people like him and he knew how to groom children so that he could abuse them. That's what paedophiles do. He took me to London once with my second cousin and he bought me an album from HMV and some loafers. He knew just how to make me feel special. But as time went on, I didn't feel special. I hated myself, I hated his attention, I hated him.

There were no boundaries at home with my mum either. There was no lock on the bathroom and, for many years, no TV in the living room. If I wanted to watch it I had to go into Fay and George's room, which always made me feel vulnerable. Bedrooms were full of nightmares for me, both real and dreamed. We were now living on a council estate in Croydon and the house was immaculate, nicely furnished and neat as a pin. To the outside world it may have all looked perfect. We had beautiful Italian furniture, crystal chandeliers and the best plush shagpile carpets – but

I had no door on my bedroom. I nailed up a curtain to the door frame when I was a teenager just to try and give myself some privacy. No one had any idea of the rage that roared in that house behind closed doors. Fay gave a good impression of a caring mum. We always had plenty of food on the table, clean clothes, a nice home. What it lacked was love.

Even when the signs of abuse were there, they were ignored. I went to school once after Fay had given me a particularly vicious beating on my shins with a piece of wood. My legs were covered in livid purple bruises, which I hid with long socks, even though it was the middle of summer. A teacher noticed my bruises during PE and asked me what on earth I had done.

A friend said, "Her mum beats her up." So all my friends must have known. Neither the teacher nor I said anything but I remember thinking, *When I get home they are going to come and rescue me, take me away from her*. But, of course, they didn't. Again, this would not have been ignored now, with safeguarding in place.

I found out much later that my stepdad had been there and witnessed that particular beating, and his friend was appalled that George did nothing to stop it. As I knew only too well, I was on my own. I coped by zoning out, taking my head to a different place while the abuse was happening. I'd get a good beating and the next day go to school as if everything was normal. To me, it was normal. Getting beaten black and blue by my mum was a just a regular part of my life.

Sundays became the day when Fay singled me out for her special brand of motherly attention. It was my mum's one day off from work and she spent most of it gearing herself up to belting the living daylights out of me. Without fail, Fay would find a reason to blame and shame me and there was no one to stop her assaults. My siblings were all frightened witnesses to this brutal Sunday ritual. I wasn't the only one living in fear of the moment Fay would start on me. We had all come to expect and dread the moment when Fay would send my siblings into another room. My sister Delaine remembers how scared they all felt for me. She recalls hearing my screams, my sobs as Fay abused me. As I grew into a teenager, these sobs stopped and anger took over. Any love I once felt for my mum was gradually beaten out of me.

To begin with, I soothed myself by comfort eating and then making myself sick. Then, when I was around 11, I started smoking and would nick my mum's cigarettes and dog ends. Before long I had moved on to glue sniffing, which was quite a big thing at that time. I bought it at the hardware store, using the money that I'd been given for my lunch. For about a year, I was just the kid that got high. It got so bad that, when I wasn't skiving off school, I would sometimes even sniff glue in the classroom while the teacher was at the blackboard. I needed to be off my face in order to cope with what was going on at home and at my nan's.

My other, less self-destructive release was music. At around the same time as the glue sniffing, I got into ska and two-tone, bands such as the Beat, The Specials, Selector. I had an asymmetric haircut and really felt as though I was part of that musical movement of the 1980s. It was wonderful escapism and such an important part of my survival. Over at my nan's, I would spend hours and hours with headphones on, listening to Tony's extensive record collection (or vinyl as you would say now). Immersing myself in the likes of Dolly Parton, The Fureys, Loretta Lynn, I would feel peaceful and calm. Music helped me find myself again and gave me a space to dream. I remember listening to Dire Straits' Romeo and Juliet and dreaming of a love story with a happy ever after. It seemed so out of reach to me as a deeply unhappy, deeply traumatised 11-year-old. Little did I know that one day I would achieve that dream with my very own Geordie soulmate.

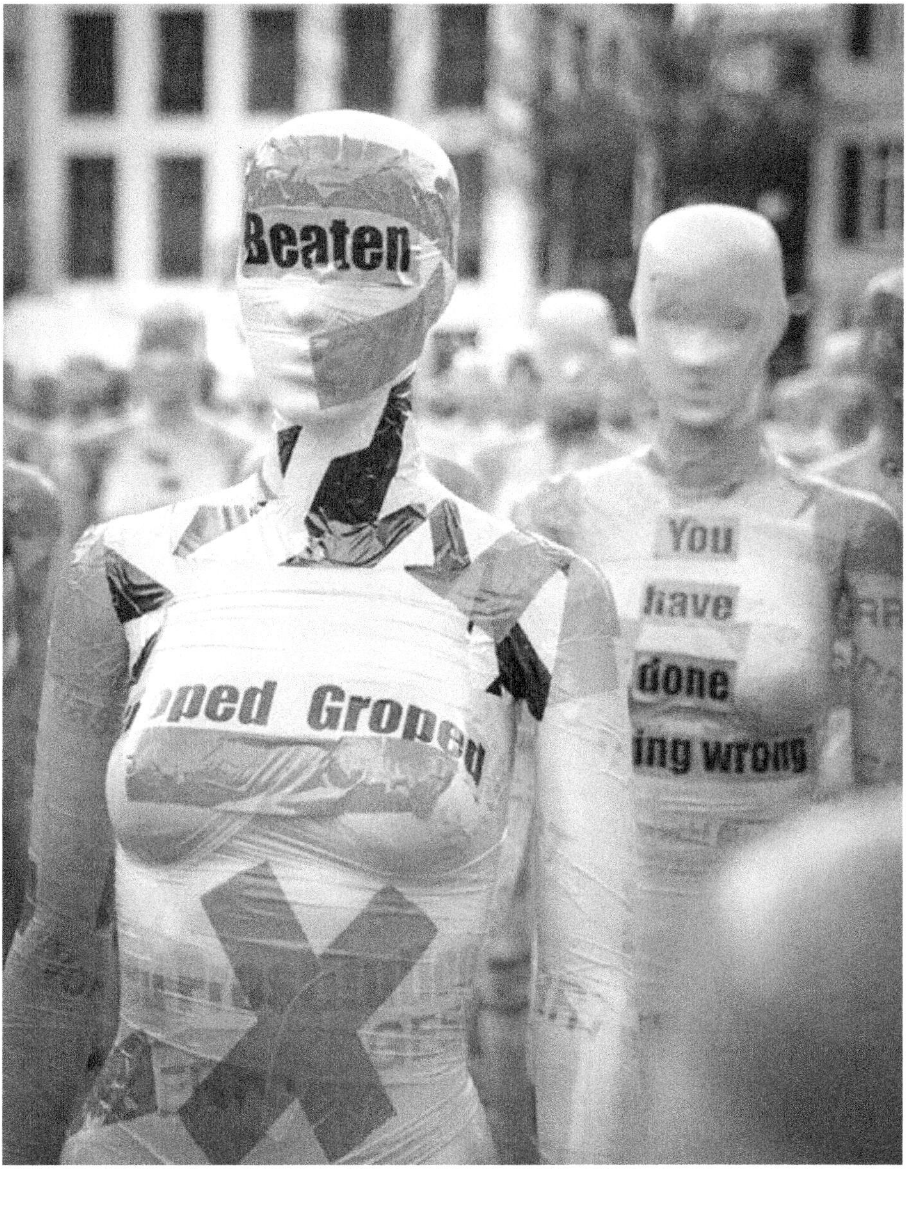
Beaten
oped Groped
You
have
done
ing wrong

5

ALONE

Soundtrack: UB40 Present Arms album, The Police, Earth, Wind and Fire, Kool and the Gang, Human League, ELO, Soft Cell, Jon and Vangelis, Aneka – 'Japanese Boy'

They are at it again. At first it's my mum hurling obscenities at George, then she moves on to hurling objects – heavy glass ashtrays go flying and now she's smashing things, smashing the door with the Hoover nozzle. George is shouting at her to stop but she carries on like a caged wild animal. Nothing will stop her. The screaming and swearing seems to go on for hours until I can tell he has his hand over her mouth, or at her throat, trying to throttle her. "Go on! Fucking do it!" screams Fay. In my bedroom, where I can hear everything through the curtain, I am silently screaming the same thing: "Just do it!"

Fay and George had brutal rows so often that I was no longer shocked by them. Their fights were vicious and neither one of them would back down. Even when George was tightening his grip around my mum's throat she would not stop screaming at him. As I lay listening to it, I was frightened that George would have to kill her to make her stop. And at the same time, that's what I prayed for. I remember many nights when I would be willing him to shut her up, to stop her, stop the noise, stop the voice, stop everything. In my head I was screaming for her to die. I just couldn't stand it any longer.

It has only just occurred to me that my brother Jeff was in the bedroom next to me, so he heard everything, too. He was six years younger than me, so heaven only knows what effect it has had on him. Their rows would go on well into the night and then we would have to get up the next morning to go to school.

There were many nights when I dreamed about running away from the mad house and the mad woman. Then one day, I actually did it for real. I used to take the weekly washing to the laundrette, lugging the heavy bag from our house and through the estate. The journey back to the house was even harder because the washed clothes were still wet and so much heavier. It was a real struggle just to lift it and I had to keep stopping along the way. On this particular day, the black bag must have caught on something and so by the time I got it home there was a rip in it. So Fay went off, calling me the C-word, telling me I was useless. As far as Fay was concerned I could never do anything right. But this wasn't a telling-off, it was pure unfiltered rage. I blocked out her ranting voice, I dissociated, because my brain couldn't cope, I couldn't stand it. I walked out of the house and decided I was never going back.

I walked and walked, eventually ending up at my friend's house. I told her I was running away and she said, "I'm coming with you." She had no reason to run away but she came with me anyway. The whole estate was out looking for us and that's when someone told my mum I had been glue sniffing and suggested that maybe I was in one of those 'glue sniffing dens'. I didn't even know such places existed. I did all my glue sniffing alone.

We spent the night in a shed and the next day my friend went home. I just walked around aimlessly, finding myself back near our old flats. I must have just gravitated to an area I knew, I didn't know where else to go. After one of George's friends saw me, my stepdad turned up in his car and said, "Get in." I did.

At that moment I had an overwhelming feeling that this was my life, that there would be no escape from this unrelenting misery. When I arrived home I was expecting a beating, but Fay just told me to go to bed. She'd been up all night and was probably too tired to lift her fists to me.

I was stuck in hell at home, feeling as though I was going insane. I was so lonely and so, so unhappy. Even going to my nan's house no longer seemed the warm refuge it once was. I was growing up and as I began to develop into a young woman, Tony's sexual abuse became unbearable. When I started my periods, at 11 or 12, I hated it. It made me feel awful about my body because I was having to wear sanitary pads that were as thick as mattresses. Tony came into the back bedroom one day when I was particularly vulnerable because I was on my period. When he removed my sanitary towel so that he could touch me, I knew that a line had been crossed. There was no part of me, as a girl or young woman, that could not be touched and now he'd even seen my insides. It was humiliating and I felt so dirty. It had to stop.

It was around this time that I told Susan, one of my school friends, that Tony was touching me. I don't think I went into detail but I was obviously serious enough that my friend said, "You've got to tell your mum." I told her that I couldn't, that Mum would kill me. Susan didn't know how bad it was at home with Fay, so she couldn't know that I feared for my life, literally. But she said, "You've got to, I'll come with you."

We went to Mum's work at Sainsbury's Homebase where she was quite high up and trusted, probably a manager. What no one knew was that this saintly woman was also organising people to steal from the store, so we had a house full of nicked stuff. My mum came out to see us and Sue urged me to tell her about Tony, but I couldn't.

Sue said, "It's Tony, he's touching her."

Mum looked at me and just said, "Go home."

I was terrified, but told my friend she should go back to her own house. She said she was staying with me. So we both went home and I waited for the bomb to explode. I honestly thought that my mum would kill me. I thought she would call me a liar and hit me and keep hitting me. But she didn't. When Fay arrived home she did not scream, or shout, or call me a liar. She did not lose her temper for one simple reason: she knew I was telling the truth.

"I believe you," said Fay, to my complete surprise. I couldn't understand how this could be happening. Then Fay said, "He's done it to me, too."

At the time I was just relieved that she believed me, I didn't even think about why my own mother would send me to my nan's, to be around a sexual predator, the man who had violated her many years earlier. It's something so heart breaking that it hardly bears thinking about, but it is something that I have had to confront as part of my recovery.

Fay took me to see her friend's husband because he was a social worker. So there I was, in a room with a man I had never met before and he was asking me what had happened. Seeing my reluctance he said, "You can tell me, it's OK." But it didn't feel OK, I didn't feel safe enough with this stranger to tell him the intimate details of my abuse.

I said, "No, it was nothing, he tried to kiss me." I was not equipped to deal with this, the after-effects of being abused, of worrying that once again I had caused trouble. I would say nothing more beyond that. My mum asked me what I wanted to do. She said we could go to the police but she framed it in such a way – my nan would have to be told and so on – that the only answer I could give was no, I didn't want to go to the police.

I have an image of myself from when I was quite young. I must have been fairly small because I was sitting inside one of those big concrete pipes in a park playground. As I sat there, my knees pulled up close, another child came and sat next to me. I must have been thinking about what went on at Nan's because I said to this other child, "A man keeps touching me, can you help me?" The child's mum was obviously horrified, I suppose he told her, and she dragged her child away pretty quickly. It makes me so sad to think of that, of my being so alone, of reaching out for help and receiving none. But I suppose it taught me a lesson, that no one outside my family could help me. And no one in my family wanted to.

So even once I had finally disclosed about Tony's abuse, my answer was no, I didn't want to go to the police. Of course I didn't. I was a child being abused by two family members. I was petrified of my mum and felt guilty that I had caused my family embarrassment by letting Tony abuse me. I felt the classic shame and blame that most survivors experience as an integral part of the effects of child abuse. I blamed myself, everything was my fault. I must be bad or why would my mum hurt me, why would he hurt me? Tony was such a nice person, it must be me. And mums don't hate their children, they don't hit, pull, scream at, punch, shove their children, because mums love their kids. I was convinced I would cause all this hate in the family if I spoke up. And the person I really couldn't bear to hurt was my nan. She would know that I had let her down, that I had done these terrible things with her husband.

As an adult I would have to live with the fact that my nan probably knew what was going on under her nose, but as a kid I assumed my nan didn't know what Tony did to me. It didn't even enter my mind. Why would it? My nan loved me. So no, I wasn't going to take it to the police. My family didn't argue with that, they didn't report him, they never checked that I was OK, they didn't get me any support. They didn't tell my dad and stepmum what had happened. No, it simply wasn't spoken about and life just carried on. For years I felt awful that I had caused an upset.

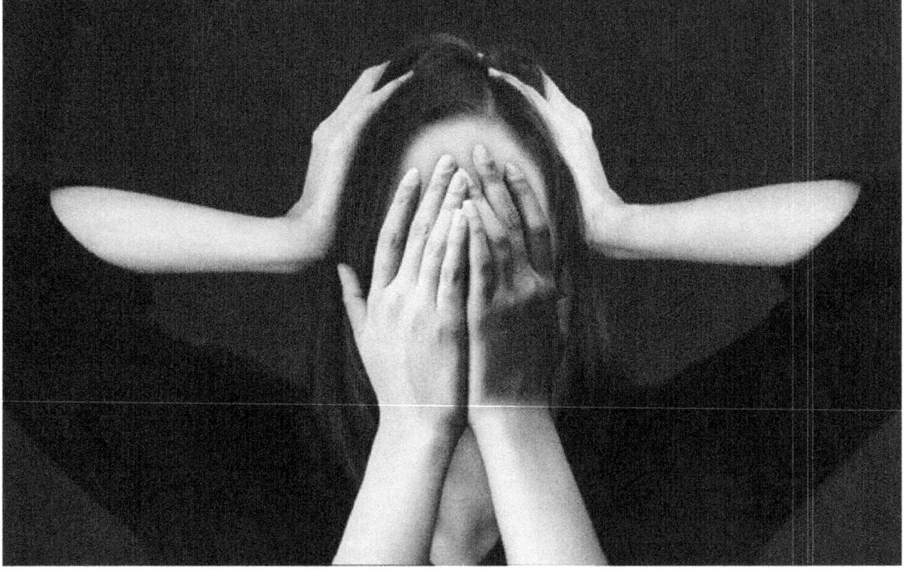

6

HEAVEN AND HELL

Soundtrack: Musical Youth – 'Pass the Dutchie', Culture Club – 'Karma Chameleon', Michael Jackson – 'Thriller', Wham, Bob Marley – 'Buffalo Soldier', Lionel Richie – 'Hello', UB40 Labour of Love album, Alison Moyet – 'That Ole Devil Called Love'

I am walking to school on a lovely sunny morning. I can breathe the clean, fresh air and I feel wonderful. I don't remember ever feeling like this, so free, so happy. I know this moment, this walk, is something I will never forget. It's magic.

It was not long after this that I got a glimpse of what a happy family life might have been. My mum had gone away to Germany for a break and when she was away I stole her family allowance book and used the money to buy records and fags. When Fay came back she noticed it was missing and asked me if I'd had it. I said no but she knew I was lying. She drew out the agony for hours, turning the house upside down and getting me to help her look for it, all the while my fear growing until finally she got the truth out of me. I imagine there would have been a beating, I can't remember now, and afterwards she called my dad and said she couldn't control me.

So I went to live with Dad and Frances and it was a magical, marvelous time. I wasn't the healthiest girl when I arrived there. I was quite overweight, thanks to all my comfort eating and I was smoking, as well as glue sniffing. But that all changed. At my dad's I no longer needed self-soothing because I wasn't anxious. Not only was I not being beaten, I was also being cared for and I was having fun. Frances cooked me special, healthy meals and made me packed lunches for school and my dad took me to the park. He would run alongside me as I rode my bike. I'd never known anything like it and it felt wonderful. At weekends we would do family things and go to see Frances's lovely sisters and their kids. I lost quite a bit of weight and felt better inside and out. I felt loved.

I will never, ever forget how magical it felt during those few months. I remember walking to school on a lovely day in spring or summer and smelling the air and just feeling happy. It makes me cry now to even think of it. I felt free and calm. I wasn't going to school stressed, I wasn't coming home to cook dinner or do chores. And I was actually being talked to. My dad and Frances weren't being nice to me to make up for the abuse I had suffered, they didn't know about it and wouldn't find out until years later. They were just being normal, loving parents. How different my life would have been if I'd lived with Dad and Frances instead of my mum.

I did go and visit Fay during that time and she would cook for me. I would see old friends in the street and realise I missed them, but I missed my brother Jeff the most. And, it's going to sound strange, but I missed the harshness of life with mum. I think it was a mixture of feeling that the hardness was what I deserved and also because my mum wanted me back with her. And when my mum wanted something she usually got it. Looking back, I realise now that it was because she didn't like me being so contented. I loved it at my dad's and I was happy. I looked different and felt different and she couldn't control me anymore. I was hers, not my dad's and she was going to take control again. So back I went, home to my mum, where I thought I probably deserved to be. It was nice to feel wanted.

When it came to my dad, Fay's jealousy knew no limits. She once told me that she had named me Louise because it was close to the name Lois, the name of Dad's girlfriend at the time Mum was pregnant with me. "He cheated on me and I wanted him to be reminded of that every time he looked at you," said Fay. I was horrified: to sully this precious thing, to name your newborn baby out of spite? If that isn't a sign of mental health problems I don't know what is.

It was jealousy that motivated my mum to do something much worse. After I returned home from my dad's, Fay sat me down and told me horror stories about him. She said that he was violent, that he'd made her have a backstreet abortion that nearly killed her, that he'd just walked away from her in hospital after she'd been given the last rites and left her to die. She also told me that he didn't really want me. So the person who had abused me daily managed to convince me that she was my protector, my saviour, while the person who I loved, who had showed me nothing but kindness, was a horrible man. Fay said that she'd never stop me seeing my dad, that I didn't have to choose between them but I knew that wasn't true. I did have to choose and I had to choose her, otherwise who knew how she would punish me. Besides, she was taking time to talk to me, to show me that she cared about me and she never did that. I was so scared of her but also craved her love and acceptance and gratefully grabbed on to any attention she showed me. So Fay got what she wanted: I barely spoke to Dad for 30 years from that moment on. What she'd told me about him was fabricated but I wouldn't find out until she'd stolen all those years from us.

I couldn't bear life back at home, even though I'd been missing Jeff and my friends. Fay gave me a short break from violence after I'd disclosed about Tony, but it wasn't long before she started hitting me again. There was one time, when I was about 13, she smashed a CB (Citizens band) radio in my face. I loved that radio because it enabled me to talk to lots of other people over the airwaves. She hit me so hard with it that it cut my eye and even Fay looked worried.

I avoided going to my nan's for about six months after I disclosed, but then I started going again, I think because my secondary school was near her. Mum always sent me to schools some distance from home, which isolated me because I had no school friends near our house. Isolation is something that a lot of abusers rely on.

So I ended up going to my nan's for lunch on schooldays. It felt very different, I felt like a very bad person for causing this awfulness. But my nan was just the same with me, if she blamed me she certainly didn't show it. We didn't really talk about it. I couldn't bear to look at Tony, or even be in the same room as him.

I was so very lonely. As well as the eating, smoking and glue sniffing, I found new ways to soothe my internal distress. I started going for walks in the middle of the night. I would sneak out of the bathroom window and walk along Purley Way, just trying to escape the pain. I was so restless and unhappy. I didn't have a plan, I would just walk and walk and then go home. I was so lucky that a car didn't stop. In that situation it would most likely have been a perpetrator if it wasn't someone who wanted to take me to the police. I would have accepted a lift with a random stranger without hesitation, gone with them wherever.

I also started going into bars and drinking on my own. I was barely a teenager, sitting on a bar stool alone and drinking gin. I probably only had enough money for one. I didn't talk to anyone and luckily no one tried to approach me. I was so vulnerable. This solitary drinking carried on for a couple of years. Alison Moyet's 'That Ole Devil Called Love' is a song I associate with those times spent propping up the bar. I remember one night having drunken sex with a cab driver. I placed no value on myself, or my body, I was easy. This is not normal behaviour. Thirteen-year-old girls don't go out on their own at night to walk the streets, or drink gin alone in a pub. My brain must have been going haywire, although to the outside world I presented as a happy girl. I had a lot of friends at school (when I was there, I skived off a lot) and was very good at masking the chaos inside me. Given the risks I took, how vulnerable and chaotic I was and the lack of value I placed on myself, I am lucky that I am still here. At the time I felt anything but lucky. I was lost.

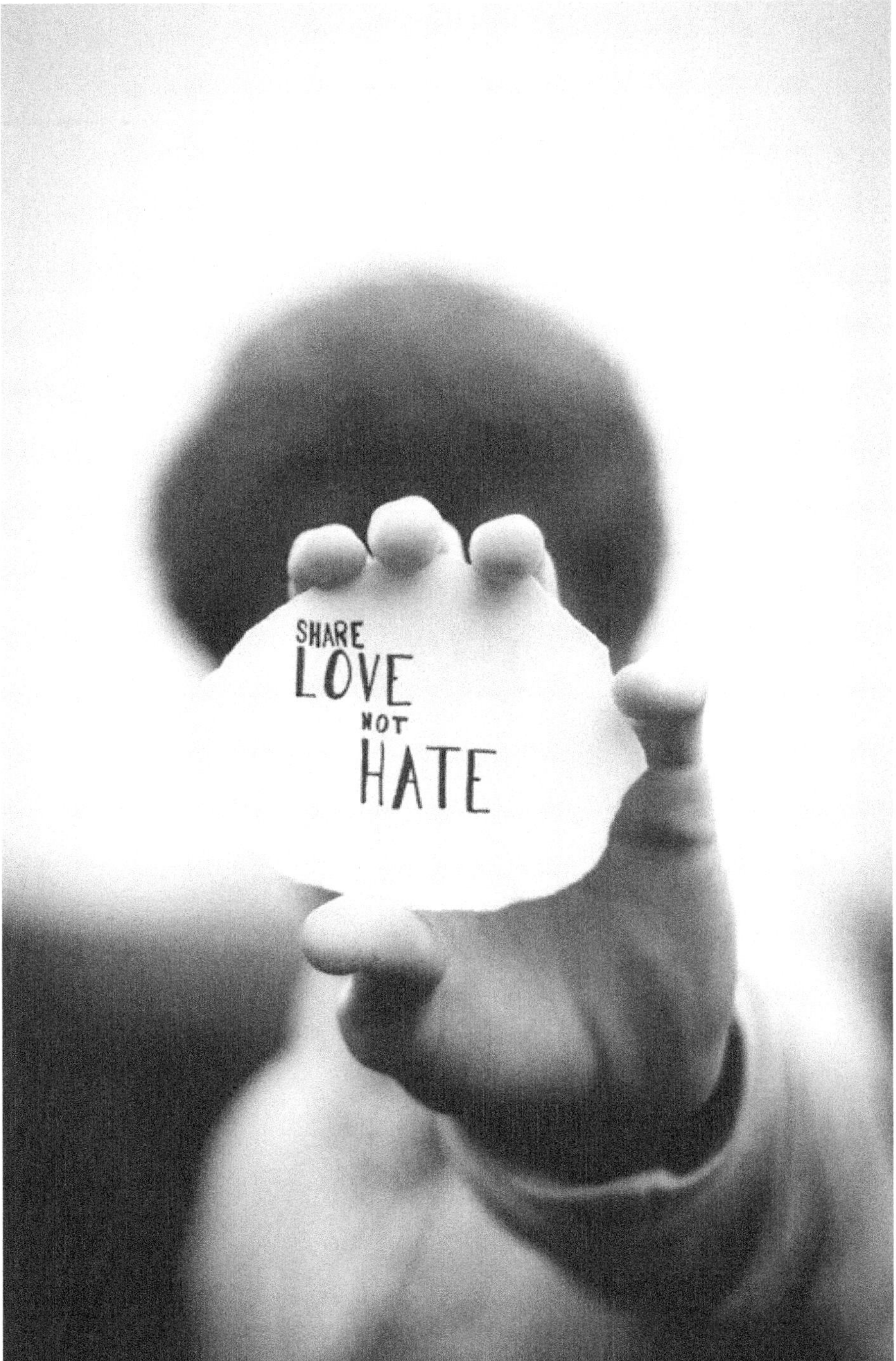
SHARE
LOVE
NOT
HATE

7

ESCAPE

Soundtrack: The Commodores – 'Night Shift', Salt-N-Pepa – 'Push It', Belinda Carlisle, Thomson Twins, Madonna, George Michael – 'Faith', Sade, T'Pau, Bon Jovi, Alexander O'Neil, Luther Vandross, The Waterboys, Peter Gabriel, Whitney Houston, Billy Ocean, Rick Astley

Fay punches me in the face and, for the first time, something in me snaps. I push her and she falls over the coffee table into the wall. She gets up and comes towards me. My heart is pounding out of my chest and I think, Shit, I'm dead.

I was 16 and it was my last day of school. I had come home and cooked dinner, making sure that I'd sent my boyfriend home and the kitchen was spotless before Mum arrived back from work. By this time I had a much better relationship with George and I'd even started to call him Dad after my mum had persuaded me that my real dad was a bastard. I had, at last, started to feel like part of the family.

But I wasn't allowed to enjoy this new sense of belonging for long: it was about to be destroyed by my mum. Fay must have come home in a bad mood. She spotted my cardigan hanging over the back of a chair and it sent her into a full-on rage. She started screaming at me about the cardi and then punched me in the face. I'm not sure what made me retaliate for the first time ever, I think it was just a reflex to get her away from me. It was just a push, but it was made worse by the fact that she fell over the coffee table. When she got up, she went ballistic and launched herself at me, punching and hitting me. She was so out of control that George rushed in from the kitchen and dragged her off me. This also enraged Fay.

"She's my fucking daughter!" she screamed at George. They argued for a bit and then Fay went up to my room, packed my bag and threw it downstairs, yelling "Fuck off!"

I took my bag and left, Fay and George still fighting in the background. Sometimes, I stop and ask myself how all this could be true. For all that drama, all that violence to have been caused over nothing, a cardigan? Surely I must have done something serious to provoke her outrage. But no, I really hadn't. It wouldn't have been the first time that Fay kicked off over nothing at all, nor the first time she had told me to go and not come back. But this time was different, it felt more final. I didn't need telling twice.

I didn't give any thought to Jeff, the little brother I left behind. He was only ten but I couldn't help him. I didn't have the capacity to think about where he was, what he must have heard, if he was going to be OK. My mental health was so poor then. I was drinking, smoking, overeating and purging, stealing food and having sex with anyone who showed me attention. I was in my own world, in survival mode. I had no time or space to think of my younger brother, I was on an operation to save my own life. My beautiful brother is now a great guy in his 40s and one of the wonderful men in my life. He has his own story of bullying and control, abuse and humiliation.

So off I went, leaving ten-year-old Jeff with Fay and George. I had often wanted to escape that house, now I had my chance. I wasn't sure where I could go. I didn't even think about going to my dad's: Fay had poisoned that relationship for me. First I went to my boyfriend's house and his mum was quite shocked to see the black eye that was coming up on my face.

"My mum did this," I said. I think it was the first time someone had seen my wounds after a beating and I had told them the truth about how they got there. I felt humiliated and stupid admitting that my own mother had beaten me up. I left my boyfriend's house and went to my friend Cheryl's. Cheryl lived on another estate not too far away and I used to go and stay there at weekends sometimes. Her mum was Spanish, mad as a hatter and absolutely lovely. Some nights, when Cheryl went out, I would stay in and talk to her mum and older brother. Cheryl was gorgeous looking and sometimes when I went out with her, I didn't feel good enough, though Cheryl never made me feel like that. She remains a good friend to this day and I am proud to be godmother to her middle daughter Abbie, who's now 21.

It was Cheryl's last day at school, too, so she was going out to celebrate, like any healthy, happy, normal 16-year-old. While she was out having fun, I was lying on her bedroom floor, nursing my black eye and feeling numb. Her bedroom was the exact opposite of mine. She had make-up and clothes all over the floor and it was so messy that I had to clear a space just to be able to sleep there. This in itself was quite traumatic for me because another of my coping mechanisms was to tidy and clean. My own bedroom was spotless, not a thing out of place, not a hint of dirt. Polishing, dusting and rearranging my bedroom gave me some sense of control and some temporary calm for my chaotic mind.

I stayed at Cheryl's that night and the next day my mum phoned up. I thought she was ringing to say sorry, come home, but instead she said, "I want my fucking keys." It was so cold, so callous and I was stunned. But I needed to focus on survival. I went to the transport café on our estate where I'd been working part-time and they agreed to give me a full-time job. I stayed at Cheryl's for another couple of nights but her bedroom was tiny and I needed to find something more permanent. Once again my survival instinct kicked in. I went round to see Debbie, a friend from secondary school who lived with her dad. I liked her dad and I asked him if he'd let me rent their spare room. I told him I would pay him rent, £20, which was quite a lot of money at the time, a large chunk of my wages. And he agreed.

So for a year I rented the spare room and went to work. I had started out making tea in the cafe, but it was so terrible that customers couldn't drink it. Then they tried me on cracking eggs – also no good – but I was pretty good at cleaning and clearing the tables. No surprise there!

I managed to leave school with eight GCSEs, which is amazing considering how often I wasn't there. I hadn't ever really given any thought to what I wanted to do with my life, what I wanted to achieve. I didn't have any hopes or ambitions for myself, I never thought that far ahead. I never had career conversations with Fay and she always put me down so I didn't have any confidence in myself. That's why I felt it was so important that I encouraged my boys to believe they could be anything and do anything they set their hearts on, just so long as they were happy. I always told them to reach for the stars.

My 16-year-old self was just happy to have a job that enabled me to be independent for the first time. My independent living came to an abrupt end when I was nearly 17 and was caught shoplifting. I stole a hairbrush. I didn't need a hairbrush, I had loads of them. Looking back I was clearly acting out, one of my self-destructive coping mechanisms. The police didn't ask too many questions, they just wanted to know why I was living on my own at such a young age. Fay came to bring me home and once I was back, if felt as if something had shifted between us, she never hit me again. But there are many non-physical ways to abuse people, as I also discovered with my first serious boyfriend.

I had started going out with him when I was 16. He had come in the café with his friend and I thought he was gorgeous, with his dark hair swept over and his smart suit that looked as though it came from Savile Row. He looked a bit like one of the Kray twins and although he was shy, he had that air about him, the sort of charisma that I saw in my mum and her brothers. That wasn't the only thing he had in common with them. I couldn't believe that this dishy guy was interested in me. Once we started going out, there was something else that drew me to him: he hated Fay. One day he said to me, "I can't stand your mother." I asked him what he meant and he said, "She'll never touch you again because I'm here." I loved that about him, that he wasn't afraid of her and would protect me, it was such a draw for me. He knows who you are, Mum. Perhaps this was because he recognised part of himself in her. But unlike my mum, whenever he was horrible to me, he would say sorry and give me flowers. And he told me he loved me, which is something I hadn't heard before. It was wonderful. I loved him. But I had just swapped one controller for another.

My boyfriend didn't hit me but he became abusive in other ways. He would try to isolate me from my friends and was very possessive. There was a lot of "Who was that you were talking to?" and he would accuse me of looking at people and cheating on him. It got to the point when I would flinch if he moved quickly, which he did deliberately in order to scare me. He put me down a lot and fear was instilled in our love. He employed all the classic shitty tactics and gaslighting that perpetrators like to use.

I left the café and after a stint as a chambermaid, got a job in a paper factory. I loved it there, the people were so nice and I was making friends. It was a fun, social time and I felt that my personality was beginning to come out. Needless to say, my boyfriend didn't like me going out drinking or having a good time with them. One time I was at our work's Christmas drinks in a pub. I had a fantastic evening, surrounded by lovely people young and old, and for once my drinking had nothing to do with my abuse or feeling lonely. We all left the pub and we were saying goodbye to one another when my boyfriend came over. He was completely drenched because he had been standing outside the pub all night.

"I've been fucking watching you," he said, his face like thunder. My friends told him to leave me alone, but I said it was OK and sent them away. I tried splitting up with him a few times and he would become aggressive and wait for me outside work. I always went back to him even though I was scared of him. I suppose, growing up with Fay, fear and love were a familiar combination.

Back at my mum's house, I knew I was on borrowed time. Fay had told me in no uncertain terms that I needed to find my own flat and I agreed with her. I started buying cutlery and pans and eventually found a bedsit to rent. Fay had told me she needed me to go because she wanted my room as an office, but in fact she was moving in my stepsister Delaine.

I was looking forward to having my own place, I had even bought my first settee, and I left home on moving day feeling very excited. At some point that day I had to return to Fay's and that's when I discovered that Delaine had already been moved in. It was a case of one out, one in. It had obviously all been arranged but nothing had been said. That was the way Fay operated. She made herself the centre of the family, the one everyone relied on and then she used that position to leave someone out. There was always a person on the outside, often me, but later on there would be others with their nose pressed to the window. It shouldn't have surprised me that I had been replaced: with me gone, Fay needed someone else to control. But the speed of it was painful. When I went home that day and discovered Fay already playing happy families with Delaine, it was as though I had never been there, I didn't exist. It was yet another reminder of how unimportant I was to my mum.

I loved my new-found freedom. I was driving by then and Fay had bought me a car. That was the generous side of my mum, the side that I seldom saw. At work in the factory I would laugh and joke, then at home in my bedsit I could do what I wanted – drink, play my music, smoke pot. I didn't take my independence for granted, it seemed wonderful to me that I was having fun and felt so free. My boyfriend's controlling behaviour didn't stop, however. When I moved from my bedsit into a house in Thornton Heath, he practically moved in with me and it was very claustrophobic. He never had a job but pretended he did. He went out every weekday morning, as if going to work, but I found out later he just walked around all day until it was time to come home. He was most probably claiming benefits from his mum's place. I became more isolated from my factory friends, just as he wanted and then I became pregnant. I think I wanted a baby to fill the loneliness inside me but I had a miscarriage at three months.

During this time I took some comfort and advice from an older woman who I worked alongside at the factory. Rhonda always had great words of wisdom and I was at her house when I miscarried. For the short time I knew her she was a protective mother figure to me. I don't think she ever realised the strength she gave me as she helped me understand what my boyfriend was doing. I realised I couldn't stand his controlling behaviour any longer and I finished with him for good. He wasn't going to go easily and in the end I had to take out an injunction to keep him away from me. His brother had assaulted Fay when she tried talk to him about the baby and the attack was reported, leaving me feeling responsible for my mother. My controller boyfriend had gone and Fay had taken on the role of rescuer. On my own again, I filled the space with parties, drinking, food and sex. Anything to fill the emptiness inside me.

8

FALLING ON VELVET

Soundtrack: Patsy Cline – 'Crazy', Neneh Cherry – 'Manchild', Fairground Attraction – 'Perfect', Yazoo – 'The Only Way is Up', Phil Collins, Tracy Chapman, Neil Young, Elton John, Kate Bush, Lynnard Skynyrd, Guns and Roses, Pink Floyd, Robert Palmer, Terence Trent D'Arby, Aerosmith, Sting, Rod Stewart, Soul II Soul, Sinead O'Connor

The blond Geordie at the bar is asking me something, but I can't work out a word he's saying. It feels a bit like trying to understand Auf Wiedersehen Pet. "He's asking if you want a drink," explains my friend Viv. "Oh," I say. "I'll have a gin and orange please." I don't buy myself another drink all night.

When I met Viv my life changed forever. I can honestly say I wouldn't be who I am today without that wonderful woman. I met her for the first time in 1987. After I split with my boyfriend, my friends and I started going to pubs in different areas. Pubs were buzzing then, it was a time of plenty when everyone had money. If you wanted to, you could spend all day in the pub, then go out for a meal, get a cab home and still pay your bills. One night we walked into a pub in Oval Road, near East Croydon station, that was popular with local workers. And there was this woman, this good-looking, smartly dressed dynamo with short blonde hair. Everyone in the pub knew Viv and to know her was to love her. If Patsy Cline's 'Crazy' came on the jukebox, chances were that someone had put it on for Viv and everyone sang along to her favourite song. I know I'll never meet anyone like her again.

Hilarious, feisty and full of warmth, Viv was a one-off. She taught me so much about the importance of kindness, of accepting people for who they are and not being judgmental. She helped so many people. There used to be a lot of drug addicts who came in the pub selling things and she'd ask them, "What you got?" She would always buy something, which earned her the nickname Del Boy. She did it to try and help keep them out of trouble. Viv would always look them in the face, really look at them, and ask how they were. She really wanted to know. Viv couldn't stand injustice and if trouble kicked off in a pub and someone got hurt, she wouldn't turn away like most people, she would say, "Are you OK? Do you need somewhere to stay?" You wouldn't want to get on the wrong side of Viv, she could be ferocious, a little Barry McGuigan, if she thought something was not right.

She was also a shining example of compassion and, unlike my mum's so-called charity, it was authentic and came from the heart. Viv's the reason I never pass a homeless person without looking them in the face and finding out how they are. Sometimes I ask them, "How did you get here?" Each person has a story and mostly that story includes abuse. They are not just homeless or drug addicts, they are people and the distance between me and them is very small. I learned about humanity from Viv.

Although there was a 20-year age difference between us, Viv and I became great friends and remained friends for many years until she died. She could be a pain in the neck sometimes, but we never fell out and we used to laugh so much. She showed me a kindness I had never really experienced and I felt she accepted me and loved me for who I was. We had so many great discussions about life (mostly drunken admittedly), but she was one of the few people whose house I would visit stone-cold sober – which shows the trust and confidence I felt around her. Viv's friends became mine and I became part of a close-knit group. When I think about that time it fills me with such warmth. I was happy and laughing, meeting the most crazy, wonderful people and having lots of parties. There's no doubt that meeting Viv was a turning point in my life – not least because she introduced me to Derek.

There are things I will never forget about the year 1988. Fairground Attraction's 'Perfect' was in the charts, there was a 70th birthday concert for Nelson Mandela, and I met some Geordie brothers who remain the most wonderful men I have ever known. Viv introduced me to Derek and his three brothers in the pub. They were all window cleaners with their own business and I could tell straight away that they were good blokes – even if I couldn't understand a word they said! Gentle, kind and good fun, they were the sort of men who didn't swear in front of women out of respect and who could have a laugh without being aggressive. This was so different from the men I'd been used to. Derek says he was attracted to me straight away, but romance hadn't really crossed my mind at this point. For some reason I always thought I would end up with someone dark haired, a south Londoner, possibly with tattoos. Not a slim, fair-haired northerner with a nose that looked as if it had been in a fair few fights (a Geordie nose I call it!).

Then I had a house party and Derek came with everyone else from the pub. He was sitting on one of my speakers, which really annoyed me.

"Do you have to do that?" I asked. He slid off without saying a word and I don't think we spoke again all night. The next morning I found his younger brother Gary asleep in my Hoover cupboard. He was full of apologies and asked if I was going to the pub. I looked around at all the morning-after mess. "Not yet," I said.

Once I'd cleaned up all traces of the party I went to the pub, where I found Derek. We got talking and I discovered how lovely he was. Even then, I wasn't exactly flirting with him. I thought he looked like a mass murderer and told him, but it didn't stop him asking me out on a date. We went for a Chinese and had a lovely night, ending up back at my house, then more drink and music. You couldn't blame Derek for not realising how nervous and cautious I was around men; buoyed up by plenty of drink I was chatty and bubbly. Even I didn't realise how anxious I was – until I did. It was very late and we were still drinking and I suddenly looked at Derek and thought, *Shit, he's here in my house. He's big and muscly and he will probably expect sex and I don't even really know him.*

As these thoughts ran around my head I went into full-on panic mode and woke up my lodger Simon. Poor Simon. He had rented a room from me after he had left his wife and I hadn't realised how having a man in my house would trigger me and make me anxious. I felt as though I didn't have any control in my own home so I started leaving notes for Simon, please don't do this, or that. Poor Simon, he was such a lovely bloke. Living with his wife must have seemed so easy compared with me!

Having woken him up, I told Simon he had to go and get rid of Derek. "How?" he asked.

"I don't know, tell him my husband's coming back, anything. Just do it, or you're out," I threatened. Sorry Simon.

So he dutifully went downstairs and told Derek he had

to go. "Her dad's coming back and he doesn't like Lou having men here," Simon improvised. "He's a very big guy, so you'd better go." While Derek left, Simon probably started making plans to move out as soon as possible, and I went into meltdown. I couldn't believe I could have been so stupid as to put myself in that situation. *He looks like a mass murderer,* I reminded myself. Yes, OK, he was kind and gentle and lovely to be with, but even so…

Viv laughed her head off when I told her what had happened. Of course she didn't know anything about my past. "You are an idiot," she said. "He is such a lovely guy." I felt awful and decided I would cook him a meal to make it up to him. He was at the bar and so I went up to ask him, but at the same moment a woman came and put her chair down next to him and Derek looked at me as if to say, 'Not now.' I was furious, the deal was off. Then Viv explained that the woman was his ex, she kept hanging around him and he was too nice to send her away.

After all that, we finally got together. I cooked him the meal and then we started to spend a lot of time together. We laughed and drank and had fun. It was a wonderful time. I was young, I had a lovely partner and we were surrounded by good, non-abusive people. Everyone in the pub joked that we were married. We had only been together six months when we did decide to get married. I don't know if there was a proposal. To be entirely honest, I wasn't in love, I'm not sure that I was capable of it at that time. I just thought this is a lovely guy and this may never happen to me again.

I hadn't seen much of my mum for a while. She had Delaine to control so she wasn't really interested in what I was doing. But once Derek and I decided to get married, Fay took over. She arranged everything, the food, the invitations, the flowers. She put a lot of work into it, I don't want to take that away from her, but I didn't really have a say in anything. Fay even made my wedding dress, sewing on pearls and beads by hand. Her aim, she said, was to try and make me look slimmer. I didn't have much confidence at the best of times, but Fay always found a way to put me down.

For years afterwards, I kept the dress in a box under my bed. I realised recently that I had never, not once, opened up the box and thought, *Here is my beautiful dress that made me feel gorgeous on my special day with my special husband.* The truth was I had never liked it, didn't feel beautiful in it on the day and hated myself in my wedding photos. I had a really strong urge to throw the dress away, this symbol of my mum's power and control that played out over my entire life. I battled with my guilt for a bit, then, earlier this year, I finally got rid of it. I chucked the dress in the bin and then threw my dinner on it. I didn't feel bad about it, I felt lighter and relieved. It had only taken me 30 years to do that!

We got married in September, in a church near where we lived and I was so pleased Viv and all my wonderful new friends were there, as well as my family. One of the songs we chose for the wedding was 'Sorry' by Tracy Chapman because both Derek and I loved it. George gave me away, which I was happy about because at that point I put him on a pedestal and we had a father-daughter relationship. The one thing I did ask for was that my dad and Frances should be on the top table. I still wasn't really talking to my dad, but he was still my dad. Fay wouldn't even entertain it. She said, "I've done everything for you and if you have him on the top table, I won't be there." Once again she made me choose between them and of course she won. I just couldn't have a voice, I couldn't say, this is my wedding and I'll do what I want, invite whoever I want. My dad's side of the family were not invited, just him and Frances. The invitation said, 'George Langley invites' and Fay said to me at the time, "Just wait till your dad sees this." She never wasted an opportunity to try and punish him.

On the day, I think I behaved towards my dad just as my mum expected and wanted me to. I was cold, didn't include him or speak to him and on the wedding video he just looked lost. How I regret my behaviour now. I feel so sad about it and I wish with all my heart that I could change it. To think about going to my own sons' weddings and them behaving so coldly towards me, well I just can't imagine it. I can't change how I treated my dad that day, but he knows how sorry I am.

I was so nervous when I took my vows that I stood at the altar and laughed hysterically, the congregation must have been able to see my shoulders going. And as I stood there, I remember looking at Derek and thinking, *This is a lovely, caring man. This will be nice for the next three or four years.* I didn't question these thoughts at all, or realise that this wasn't normal thinking for a bride. I realise now that, at the time, I didn't believe in relationships working, I didn't believe in happy ever after. Derek did. Or, at least, he believed in us. He absolutely knew I was the one, the person he wanted to share the rest of his life with. It just took me a little while to catch up. And now here we are, 32 years later, and I couldn't love, respect or cherish this quietly wonderful man more. Meeting Derek was falling on velvet.

9

LOVE AND DESPAIR

Soundtrack: The Corrs, Coldplay, Dido, Eminem, David Gray, Kate Bush, Garage and Old School, Bryan Adams, Chris de Burgh, REM, Enigma, Seal, Alanis Morissette, Celine Dion, Mary J Blige, Oasis, Lenny Kravitz, The Verve, Mary Black

I am a mum. My beautiful son Billy has just been born by emergency caesarean. I am exhausted but elated, full of fear about being a mother but full of happiness that my son is here, with his mop of dark hair. My mother arrives and says to me, "You could've put some make-up on." This is Fay's response to the safe delivery of her first grandchild after a 32-hour labour: to tell me I was ugly and could have made more of an effort.

I fell pregnant with Billy a year after we were married. It had been a very happy year, when I felt safe and loved. Derek and I worked hard and played hard. There was many a sociable weekend in the pub, surrounded by lovely friends and my wonderful new Geordie family. Alcohol and music featured largely. Like me, Derek loved music – he also played guitar – and my musical tastes widened as he introduced me to different artists. Surrounded by good people, my anxiety took a back seat, but it was always there, waiting to surface.

I was delighted when I discovered I was pregnant but it also triggered all those fears, doubts and insecurities that I had managed to push down. I guess many first-time mums worry about what sort of parent they will be, but my anxiety, wrapped as it was in all my old trauma, was played out in self-destructive behaviour. I did at least stop drinking through my pregnancy, but I replaced it with food, binge eating and purging until I ballooned in size. I looked like Richard Branson's hot-air balloon! I was stuffing down my feelings. At the same time I was also stealing, never from individuals, always from shops. I was a prolific shoplifter, it's amazing Croydon had anything left on its shelves and amazing that I was never caught. Derek was a great provider and would have bought me anything I wanted, plus I worked myself so money was not an issue. I was stealing when I didn't need to and stealing things I didn't need, mainly things for the baby. It's obvious now that my past was being played out in everything I did. I felt depressed and anxious at what should have been one of the happiest times in my life.

I think I was also being triggered by the simple fact of

being loved by Derek, it felt so overwhelming and unfamiliar. This may be hard to understand, but after constantly being told by my mother how useless I was, I never really believed I was lovable. I had never been valued and it felt uncomfortable to be happy, to be loved. For all of my early life, love brought pain and anxiety. It was just going to take a while for me to realise that Derek always had his arms around me, was always holding me, keeping me safe. As for becoming a mum, I didn't exactly have the best role model.

I didn't see much of Fay during my pregnancy. She had left George for another man, the builder who was doing up her house. This wouldn't be the last time she would cause turmoil and loss by leaving her husband and son for a new man. When she arrived on the labour ward after Billy was born and told me that I should have tried harder with my appearance, I told her to go, get out of the room. I was so upset. "You could have put some make-up on." This was Fay's advice to a nervous and exhausted new mum. I hated her in that moment.

And yet, Fay had managed to convince me that she was the parent I could rely on, the only parent who loved me. I had no contact with my dad at this point, Fay kept up the fiction that he didn't love me and I believed her. I know now that children tend to side with the abusive parent. It is the only choice you can make without coming under attack.

My nan came to see me every day in hospital, bringing love and support. She was always a much better mum to me than Fay ever was. George and my brother Jeff also came to see me. I remember crying as they sat beside me because I could see the loss in both their eyes, they both looked so sad without Fay. George was not a great husband, he didn't work, didn't take Fay out or on holiday, and he just wilted without her. For a while I'd built him up to be the better of the two parents, but he wasn't. He enabled Fay and backed her up in all her abusive behaviour. But I had grown to love him dearly and felt so sorry for him as he sat there in the hospital. It was clear he couldn't exist without her. Jeff told me they had been living on eggs and chips every night since she left. My brother bore the brunt of Fay leaving. He felt abandoned and was really hurting. I could totally relate to Jeff's feelings of being unloved, but I had to shut out his pain and deal with my new baby, who was in the special care unit. Eventually Fay did return to the family home. One day she just bounced in with her newly permed hair as if nothing had happened. Fay was back, the mourning was over and we weren't to talk about it – ever!

My baby boy knew nothing of this family turmoil. He had a nan and grandad, aunties and uncles, he had love from our many friends and love in abundance from me and Derek. He was so bloody cute – a lovable, happy, cuddly beautiful boy. I didn't really like anyone else picking him up, and only really felt he was safe when he was at home with me. I could never entirely shake off my knowledge that bad things could happen to babies.

Our second son, Charlie, was born the following year, in July 1992. It was quite a stressful time as Charlie, like his big brother, had to go into the special care unit. He was a big baby, a chunky 10lb 4oz and he was the cuddliest baby ever. He had the loudest cry, like the boom of an ocean liner, but when he wasn't crying he was utterly adorable. Charlie was quite unsettled as a baby and cried a lot and I truly believe he had picked up on my depression and trauma.

I was a very anxious mother. I didn't want anyone to touch my kids. I was very anxious when we went to children's parties and I accepted invitations reluctantly. When it came to letting my toddlers out of my sight, I just couldn't do it and would make up all sorts of excuses to explain my behaviour. I wouldn't let them stay anywhere else, I didn't want them to go to any place where I couldn't keep a watchful eye on them. Even now I don't like to pick up other people's babies. I just feel they are too precious, too vulnerable to be shared. I know absolutely that these feelings are my problem, it's connected to the deep trauma I experienced. I wasn't safe as a baby or as a child, my body was public property, to be beaten or touched by my abusers. And my abusers were the people I should have been able to trust most. It's hardly surprising that, when it came to my own boys, I was full of fears for them.

In 1994, we moved back to the Mitcham estate where I grew up. Me, Derek and our two handsome, gorgeous little boys moved into a three-bedroomed council house where we were to stay for the next 17 years. I loved that house and we had some good times there. Living on that estate we were part of a community with lots of families and we all looked out for one another. I started spending a lot of time with my cousin Donna, who has been like a sister and best friend throughout my life. We shared some lovely family time as her children and mine played together. I also got to know Donna's friend Sonia, who was to play a hugely important part in my story later on. Together with my brother Jeff, who lived close by, we formed a breakfast club and our exclusive little gang of four would meet once we'd dropped off the kids at school. For all of my anxiety, I was a fun and bubbly mum and I cherished time spent with my sons, reading stories, having cuddles, singing and dancing with them. My house was full of laughter, love and happy children.

I had unconsciously moved back to the estate where, a decade earlier, I was systematically punched and screamed at, where I glue-sniffed away the pain, where I walked through alleyways crying and wanting to run away. I dissociated from all of that earlier pain and was able to create some happy family memories there with Derek and my boys. But as my sons grew older, so my anxiety about keeping them safe grew stronger. Slowly, the snake that was my trauma uncoiled itself and started to slither to the surface.

When the boys were about five and six, my mental health started to slip and the old coping mechanisms kicked in. I would overeat Monday to Thursday, go out to the pub and binge drink on Fridays and then on Saturday night I would stay in and drink with Derek. I was swimming 40 lengths a day, cleaning excessively and was always rearranging rooms, humping huge pieces of furniture around. Anything to stop myself acknowledging the fear and pain inside me. I wasn't sleeping and my hair started to fall out, so for a while I had to wear a wig. On Friday nights, if my friends weren't free I would go to the pub on my own and ease my internal distress with brandy. I would repeat the same behaviour as my disconnected 13-year-old self, with those same feelings of loneliness and helplessness. But now I could afford more than one drink and I would get so smashed sometimes that I could hardly walk. But at least I felt happy and calm and was able to initiate sex with my husband, which was difficult when I was sober. This had nothing to do with my love for Derek, this was my trauma. I was disconnecting from my body as well as my head and heart. Yet to the outside world I was happy and outgoing.

In the middle of all this, Derek's mum died suddenly and I drove up to Newcastle with Derek and his brothers, Gary and Jim. I was sitting in the back of the car with Gary who was drunk and in party mode. His brothers weren't amused but it's a journey I hold very dear because of what happened later.

Meanwhile I was regressing into my trauma and I started to withdraw from Derek. I was drifting into a space where

I focused all my worries on him. I felt we were growing apart, that he had no use for me and I was of no use to him. I was drowning in a feeling that overwhelmed me, I felt like I was nothing, useless, empty. Derek was working very hard and I was spending a lot of time with Fay and George. Most weekends I would drive over to Kent where they now lived. Yes, I was so far in denial about my past that I sought comfort from my mother, the very person who had helped to cause these feelings. That's how disconnected I was. It was a bit like Stockholm syndrome, when you love your abuser. I remember driving the kids from Croydon to Kent, with Jagged Little Pill by Alanis Morissette blasting out of the car speakers.

I didn't talk to Derek about how I was feeling. I just remember a deep sense of being alone, without realising that I had withdrawn. Then I stopped talking altogether. I was trapped in my head, deep in my trauma. I woke every day feeling totally unlovable, a useless wife, a terrible mother, a fat, ugly shitty excuse for a person.

One day I woke up and decided it was time to stop the pain, I was so unbearably tired I couldn't go on any longer. I decided to take an overdose: I had insulin and syringes in my fridge and I could just float away. Within half an hour it would all be over, all this pain. My last thought, before I drifted off, was that I must write a note for Derek to pick up the boys from school and to remind him to give them dinner. Luckily, I had drifted off to sleep, not oblivion. When I woke up, I realised that if I had not been so exhausted, too tired to go and get the insulin, Derek would have found me dead and my sons would have been without their mum.

It wasn't until 15 years later that I realised just how close I had come to dying that day. I cannot imagine the story that would have unfolded for Derek and my boys. I would have left them all thinking I was crazy and didn't love them. The thing is, Derek hadn't changed. He loved me as he always did, he worked hard to provide for our family as he always did and he was there to hold and support me as he always did. I had regressed so deeply into my past that I was unconnected to the real world. Like a soldier with PTSD when they return home safely, I was reliving my trauma day after day in my private war zone. All the emotion I had cut off as a child was there, needing to be processed and healed, I just did not know it.

I was so scared by what had nearly happened and I did finally talk to Derek about it. An appointment was made to see the GP, who gave me antidepressants which I didn't take. I think I knew subconsciously that it would simply be putting a plaster on an old wound. Anyway, I had my own plaster – binge eating and drinking. In the end, there would be no healing without me finally confronting my past, and I needed help with that.

I often wonder how my trauma and my disconnection has affected my boys. Did they sense it at the time? I feel they must have done. I think for a while I was functioning on empty. If I cut off to the world, did I cut off from them? Children adapt and are resilient but I have no idea if they ever felt what I was feeling – unloved and unlovable? My biggest reason for writing this book is to put the pieces of the puzzle together for them. I want them to understand why I am who I am because it may help them understand their own emotions should they ever find themselves feeling disconnected or lonely. Above all, I want them to know that they have always been the most loved, most precious thing in my life.

DON'T
GIVE
UP!

10

THE HEALING BEGINS

Soundtrack: Pink Floyd, Dire Straits, Kate Bush, The Verve, REM, Beverley Knight

I walk into RASASC for the first time and I am blown away. Here are beautiful, wholesome, supportive women who acknowledge that any form of violence against other women is vile and unacceptable. I have, at last, found my tribe.

In 1999 tragedy struck. Derek's younger brother Gary was murdered, stabbed to death in his home in Thornton Heath. This was a terrible, terrible loss to Derek, his two other brothers, four sisters and the whole of his family. Everyone was devastated, including me. My love for this family is immeasurable. I was blessed to be around those brothers: steady, dependable, hardworking, rugged, strong, beautiful northern men. Gary was the wildest of them all and losing him left a huge gap in everyone's hearts. It was a sad, sad time, and I held Derek with all the love I could.

I remember feeling that my sons should know the importance of this family loss, to see grief but not the anger in all of us towards the murderer who killed Gary. I was scared of that anger being passed to my sons and very protective of them not to hear it. They did, however, witness the grief in their dad and Geordie uncles, who drank down their pain and played guitars, smoked, laughed, worked and drank more to get through it. The world had most definitely lost a bit of its sparkle the day Gary died. It was the only time in our whole 32 years that I saw a tear run down Derek's face, just one solitary tear.

I deeply regret making the decision that my sons shouldn't go to the funeral and the gathering afterwards. Instead they stayed with my mum for a few days. They should have been with us all, should have seen the love in that pub. Viv and every friend of those four wonderful brothers attended. I thought that pubs and funerals were not a place for children. I was so wrong! Another heartfelt apology to both Billy and Charlie, I am so sorry for this. I sometimes think we as adults forget that children are grieving as well.

After Gary's death I gave up my job at Makro where I worked part-time as supervisor for a jewellery concession. I think I was searching for something more meaningful. I had an idea that volunteer work might give me something to focus on, while perhaps helping me feel good about myself. So I started volunteering with Home Start, a charity that supports families with children under five. My role was to offer support to mums who were struggling to cope. I loved feeling useful, loved trying to make a difference and slowly my self-esteem began to build.

Boosted by my experience with Home Start, I decided to take my English Lit A-level and passed it, which added to my growing confidence. And it was around this time, in 2000, that I walked through the door of RASASC (Rape and Sexual Abuse Support Centre) in Croydon and my life would never be the same again. I had found my tribe: these courageous, passionate, compassionate women who challenged the justice system and fought on every level for female survivors of sexual violence. I started off by volunteering on the helpline and I loved it so much that I would even volunteer on Christmas Day. Eventually I was offered a full-time job there and was out in the field, learning all the time, both through experience and from training. It meant so much to be part of this fantastic group, and to be growing in confidence and knowledge.

Obviously, a lot of this work resonated with my own experiences but I still wasn't connecting with my own trauma. How could I open up that box without going mad? It was too much. I was still pushing down my feelings, happily in denial whilst happily helping others.

Then my nan died. My lovely nan. To me she represented warmth and love, filling the gap where my mum should have been. Yet it now seems clear that, at the very least, she must have known about Tony's abuse and, in my worst nightmares, she actually enabled it.

After I disclosed about Tony, aged 12, Nan remained an important part of my life. On Saturdays we would meet outside Littlewoods in Croydon, then have lunch and go shopping together. Nan loved my boys and spent some lovely time with us at our house, getting the bus over most weeks. I have to say that Tony was never allowed anywhere near them.

Then came a time, in her 70s, when she started getting ill and she asked me to clean for her. I would go round every week, to this house where all the horrors happened and I think this was the catalyst for my depression that led to my near suicide at 28. But, in my dissociated state I didn't realise that it was making me ill to clean the bathroom where Tony touched me, and the back bedroom, and every room in that house. It was making me ill, was draining the life out of me. Again the body knows what the brain can't process.

The brain is a very clever organ and it was doing exactly what it should have been doing: it was protecting me from the horrors by shutting down. Trauma is not rational, that's why the justice system is stacked against survivors of domestic abuse and sexual violence. A woman reporting rape is expected to give her statement of what happened, but chances are she can't remember it in perfect chronological order. Nor will she be able to connect to all those feelings that may help to build her case. So she doesn't say, 'I thought

I was going to die, my body went into shock, I was terrified.' These details are so often left out by witnesses because they have been traumatised and so can only give a fragmented account – and that's why so many perpetrators of sexual violence get away with it. And that is why so many women don't report, they feel there's no point, especially when you consider that they don't let women have counselling until after the court case. These are often women who can't afford to pay for private counselling, so, shockingly, they have to sit in their trauma until after the court case, which can take up to a couple of years. They have no help to put those fragmented parts back together, which doesn't make them strong witnesses. 'I can't remember,' is not a convincing answer in court.

So yes, I did not immediately connect my growing depression with being back in my nan's house. But somewhere I must have made a link because I told my nan I couldn't clean anymore. I didn't see her for a while and gradually Nan was becoming more and more frail with dementia. She was still living in the house with Tony but was going to church every day. When I wanted to see her, I parked outside the church and waited for her to come out. She would look at me with her dementia eyes, not recognising me and would say, "I don't know who you are." It was so upsetting and I would reply, "It's Lou, remember? I saw you yesterday." Other times she would start crying and ask, "Why have you left me? I haven't seen you for years," which broke my heart. She was like a baby and I just wanted to hold her.

The last time I saw my nan was deeply emotional. Nan was now living in a care home, after suffering a bad fall. When I went to see her there, I was shocked to find her pushed in front of the telly along with all the other residents. We went to her room and I read her the letter I had written. It said I would never be sure if she knew about Tony, but that I loved her anyway, I thanked her for her kindness and love and the many cherished moments we had shared. I also had a letter for Tony that said, 'You are an abuser and you always will be and when my nan is at rest, I will still be here and you can't shut me up.' I pinned both letters on her wall along with some photos of her and me together. I held her and told her how well the boys were doing and I told her how much I loved her. It felt like closure, I knew I wouldn't, couldn't, go to see her again.

For all those years I had never wanted to hurt my nan by exposing Tony as the abuser he was. It was bad enough that I had caused so much upset within the family when I first disclosed to my mum. But once Nan died, in 2002, I felt I could finally report him to the police. I think by this point I was also in a better place mentally and emotionally, so I had the strength and courage needed to take this huge step. Feeling supported, inspired and propelled forward by the wonderful RASASC women and their courageous fight for justice, I knew it was time to get my own justice. I didn't have to do it alone. My beautiful friend Sonia came with me to South Norwood Police Station. I will be eternally grateful to Sonia for her great support when I most needed it.

It takes a great deal of courage to report any form of sexual violence: it's a very distressing and vulnerable thing to do. And the way I was treated on that day could easily have persuaded me not to pursue it. I was taken to a horrible cupboard of a room and I was interviewed by an ar**hole who clearly had no experience of dealing with abused women. He was so cold and clinical as he sat typing away, asking questions with no regard for the distress it was causing. When he asked if there were any distinguishing marks on Tony and I pictured the scar on his stomach, his tattoo, it plunged me right back in those moments of abuse. Because of my experience at RASASC, I knew a lot about reporting rape and I think that's what stopped me from walking out after 10 minutes.

Fay was irritated that I had gone to the police without telling her. "You've waited all this time and then you don't even tell me," were her motherly words of comfort. She had to give a statement about Tony's abuse, as did another family member. It took a year and a half for his case to go to court. I had seen what women were up against in court during rape and abuse cases, but I was more than ready for a fight. In the end I didn't have to go because he pleaded guilty to seven charges of indecent assault against two of us.

Seven charges! He was charged for different types of

assault, it didn't include the number of incidents over all those years. When I think of all the countless times and countless ways he touched and abused me. And who knows how many other young girls he abused over the years? My nan was a childminder during the 80s, so he had plenty of access and, as I knew only too well, he was brazen and opportunistic.

He was given a three-year sentence, which is an absolute joke. I just wish I could go and report him again, this time I would include all the pre-verbal abuse he inflicted on me as a baby, which, after intense therapy, I've only been able to talk about in recent years. To say I was disappointed with the sentence is an understatement, but at least he was going behind bars.

I went to a Croydon paper with the story. I had a headline for them, 'Local Hero Jailed As Sex Offender'. In 1999, Tony had been hailed as a hero when a man, a paranoid schizophrenic, had come into church waving a samurai sword at the congregation and Tony had stood up and blocked his way. I wanted everyone to know just what kind of man this hero was this funny, generous, sociable, churchgoing, sexual abuser of children. And I was hoping it would encourage anyone else who'd suffered at Tony's hands to come forward.

Helping to put him behind bars was another step forward towards healing. Then I started having therapy with a wonderful woman called Anne and I knew this was going to be the toughest journey of my life. Confronting all those feelings that I had managed to block for all those years was going to be intense but life changing and I knew I had to do it. As I began to process what happened with Tony, I realised just how much safer I felt now that he was behind bars. I realised how much fear had been attached to his abuse. As a little girl I must have been constantly frightened.

My learning deepened when I began studying for a Counselling degree in 2002. Through therapy, study and work, I was in a healthy place, learning a lot and becoming much more self-aware. I was understanding more about child development and slowly putting the pieces of my own fragmented past together.

Then one day I had a stark reminder that the past could always catch up with me. Charlie was 11 at the time and he was late coming home from being out somewhere. It was only 10 minutes, but it may as well have been a lifetime. I worked myself up into a dreadful panic, imagining he was lying dead somewhere, so that by the time he walked in, I was hyperventilating and in a complete state.

I screamed at him, "Where the fuck have you been?" and I pushed him. He fell against the door and his head smashed the glass. At that moment my world fell in. I saw my son's face, his shock and confusion. I told Charlie to go upstairs. I was horrified at what I'd done. "How dare you do that to your son?" I raged at myself. "You of all people know what that feels like." I had turned into my mum.

I went upstairs and Charlie was crying. I said, "Son, I can't put into words how wrong that was and I'm so, so sorry. But I will tell you that you have done nothing wrong, it's all me. I have a huge problem and I am getting help to sort it out." It was a lightbulb moment for me, realising how much damage had been caused by my own mother and how much damage I could now cause my own children if I didn't sort it out. When the boys were young, and with Fay's approval, I disciplined them with a wooden spoon, and I sometimes gave them a slap on the bottom. I am so ashamed of that now. I would be mortified if anyone slapped my grandson Davie. Thank God my son Charlie is a better parent than I was in that respect. I was so damn scared about what had happened with Charlie that day and I determined this would never happen again.

The boys knew I was in counselling and, when they were nine and ten, I had told them a little of my past, just enough for them to know I had a troubled time and that this may impact on my behaviour. As well as my private therapy, I was having counselling as part of my course. It was all helping. In the end I didn't finish my degree. After nearly four years and with two months to go, I pulled out. I had imposter syndrome. Those old feelings of insecurity were kicking in. Who did I think I was, getting a degree? I could not silence those negative voices telling me I wasn't good enough, even though all my dismayed tutors said I was and they were urging me not to leave. I realise now that I was scared of success, I didn't think I deserved it. So I pulled out and didn't get my degree, didn't go to the diploma ceremony wearing my cap and gown. There would come a time eventually when I could take pride in my achievements, but not yet.

11

RIGHTING WRONGS

Soundtrack: Leona Lewis, Usher, Stereophonics, Paul Simon, Coldplay – 'Fix You', Mary Black, Christina Aguilera – 'Stripped', Dido, Black Eyed Peas, James Blunt, Avril Lavigne – 'Nobody's Home'

There is shock and pain etched on the faces of my dad and Frances. They cannot believe what I am telling them, cannot get their heads around the awfulness. Fay has robbed us of 30 years of love, of being together. My dad breaks down and they both have tears flowing down their faces.

My childhood memories of my dad are all about warmth and love, music and fun. If I look at photographs of when I was young, he was always holding me, always cherishing me. We were so close and I loved riding my bike to go and see him and Frances, who I also loved. That had all came to an abrupt end on the day Fay sat me down in her kitchen and told me what sort of person my dad 'really' was. I remember thinking, *Wow she must really care about me to want to have this adult conversation.* She went on for ages, telling me how he had stubbed out cigarettes on her face, how he had broken her ribs. None of it was true. But my mum knew how to manipulate my feelings and she kept up this fiction about my dad for decades. And so for decades I sided with my abuser. The loss of him in my life was something I didn't think about and I put all of my love into my stepdad George. It was only later I realised that George was simply not worthy of that love, he was Fay's puppet and enabled her abuse of me. He was the calm voice of reason, so if he saw no wrong in his wife's treatment of me, no one else would question it. He backed her decisions over the years, often saying, "She did her best, she gave you everything." No she didn't! She didn't give me the one single thing that I needed – love. Fay and George did not allow truth to be spoken.

For 30 years I kept myself very remote from my dad, even when I became a mum and he became a grandfather. There was very little contact between us. I did call him after I had reported Tony for sexual abuse and he was horrified. This was the first he knew of any of it. No one had told him after I disclosed to my mum and he had been kept in the dark all this time. Little did he know, this was only the half of it. He knew nothing about the abuse I suffered at home.

Then we were brought together again by tragedy. Dad and Frances's son – my half brother – died. Dad got in touch to tell me the devastating news and I went round to see him and Frances. Even in the midst of their grief, they welcomed me just as if we had never been estranged. Slowly, our relationship started to mend. Over time, I talked to Dad and Frances about Fay and her violence, her manipulations and lies. They simply could not believe that Fay had sent me to my nan's house, knowing that Tony was a sexual predator. There was more than one occasion when Dad and Frances would just sit and cry. One day I told them what Fay had said about Dad being a bad person who had physically harmed her and didn't care about me. Their grief and shock told its own story – they couldn't comprehend how or why she would be so callous. For all those years I believed that my mum had my back and that my dad didn't want to see me.

"But that's not true!" said Frances. "Lou, we fought to see you." As for the violent abuse I suffered, my dad said he thought Fay's unhinged fury was reserved solely for him. He never imagined that a mother would unleash the same violent rage towards her own young child. Fay manipulated me for all those years but the thing is, abusers never expect you to grow up, to have a voice. And as we all know, love is so much stronger than hate. Slowly, my dad and I rebuilt our relationship. It was beautiful to have him and Frances back in my life. Dad is so full of life and laughter and Frances is an amazing, kind Irish angel. I love them both so much.

I also loved my job. At RASASC, I was training and

developing skills in the field, always propelled forward by the passion of those wonderful women who worked there. Eventually I became a bit of a specialist in sexual violence and child abuse and took on the role of Advocacy Co-ordinator. This involved supporting women and girls through medicals, acting as go-between if they decided to report their assault, as well as providing assistance before and during their trial. I was by their side right up until they first started counselling after they'd had their verdict. I also supported women and girls with historical child abuse cases. I wanted to learn as much as possible and studied hard, my brain soaking up all the information like a sponge. Through my job at RASASC, I trained as an Independent Sexual Violence Advisor (ISVA) and was posted part-time at a Family Justice Centre to work with women who had suffered domestic abuse but also additionally suffered sexual offences, such as rape. The Family Justice Centre (now called FJC) was a totally new concept because it enabled women to get all the help they needed from one place rather than having to report to many different services. It was full on, challenging, difficult and rewarding work. Progress was slow but I felt as though we were gradually winning the battle to hear victims and to give families an alternative to staying in hell. I often wonder, had these services been available to my mum, my nan, aunts and uncles, if the abuse may have skipped a generation.

Spending time focusing on victims of crime helped soothe some of my own abusive past. As well as working hard, I was still playing hard, with lots of binge drinking at the weekend. Life at home with Derek continued to be happy and I loved our Saturday nights in, when Derek and I would sit and listen to music together. Derek had introduced me to new artists, including Pink Floyd, Dido and Mary Black, but we responded to it slightly differently. Derek had grown up in a stable, happy family and he listened to music because he liked it. Whereas for me, music had always been my way of coping, my escape from reality. I would get lost in it and the words had a profound effect on me. We'd listen to some songs that would touch my heart with their beauty and connect me with my own sadness. Mary Black was a really important part of my recovery. I spent hours listening to her beautiful, pure music, and there was something in her lyrics that took me back to being a distressed, vulnerable child. I was soothed and grieving at the same time. Many a Saturday night was spent drinking and crying to music, but the kids were sleeping upstairs and I was safe with my husband. And, as always, when I cried, Derek was there to hold me. 'Fix You' by Coldplay is Derek, it's being loved, being held and falling on velvet.

I wasn't seeing much of Fay at that point, she was in and out of my life. Then, one night she turned up at our house spoiling for a fight. At this point she was no longer living with George and Jeff. She had ditched them for a second time, having started a relationship with a work colleague. She had driven for miles from Kent to make her point to me, I can't remember what that point was now but she was angry about something. No, it was more than anger, she was disturbed and very on edge. The kids were asleep and Derek was upstairs. Fay built herself up to rage very quickly, she wanted a fight and wanted me to respond. Thankfully I was very calm.

Then she said, "You want to fucking hit me don't you?" Nothing could have been further from my mind. I started to feel quite small, reduced to the young girl she had terrorised. When I said no, I didn't want to hit her, Fay suddenly started punching her own face, really hard. It was horrendous. She started moving towards me and I was aware that if I said anything at all, made any move to try and stop her, it would have resulted in her hitting me. We moved through the house, she was backing me up and still I wouldn't give her what she wanted, I wasn't responding. We got into the kitchen, all the time she was slapping herself. I was so scared and I think I went into shock. Then we got into my kitchen and she picked up a knife. And at that point I thought she was going to stab herself.

All the time she was goading me, "Come on, this is what you fucking want." My mind flashed up the various scenarios, her lying on the floor, me getting the blame. She wanted my hand on that knife, I could almost see her grabbing it to put it on there, but I was not going to give her the chance. I told her to put the knife down, shouting to make myself heard. Derek heard all the noise and came downstairs. He never raises his voice but he shouted at her to leave.

She never forgot this and in the future, she would refer to the time, "Derek chucked me out of the house," as though it was nothing to do with her. I realise now it was a full-on psychotic episode and it disturbed me to the core. It took me a long time to fully get over the shock. After all the progress I had made in my recovery, Fay could still tap into that frightened little girl inside me. I remember worrying about her driving home, along with feeling confused and distressed at what I'd just witnessed.

I didn't speak to Fay for quite a while after that. She had divorced George and the family home was sold for the second time. George was living in a caravan and wasn't in a good way, while Jeff was once again left with feelings of rejection, anger and distress. But that's what Fay did, in classic abuser fashion. She had a pattern of behaviour where she would leave for two or three years, so that everyone mourned her and missed her and longed for her to come back. And then, when it suited her, she would return like Mary Poppins. And her attitude was, 'OK, I'm back, are you all going to behave yourselves now?' And she would be welcomed back on her terms, with no mention ever made of her being away, or the other man.

After her psychotic incident, she eventually split from her new man and invited George back into the new family home. He ran back to her, like an obedient puppy. She launched her own charm offensive on me, sending little cards and kind words saying she'd love to see the boys. And there she is, back in your life, because it's easier than putting up a fight and because, despite everything, you do still want her to be there. She and George were remarried in 2008 and I suppose we were pleased to see them back together, to see some stability restored.

In the meantime, I had become a grandmother. Charlie's son Davie was born on my birthday in 2007. Charlie was just 14 when he became a dad and I think it was quite a traumatic time for him. My mum was outraged, forgetting that she was only 15 when she had me. Looking back, I don't think Charlie received much loving adult support, my family behaved like idiots, and I really saw how adults disregard children's feelings. I can't say that I wasn't worried for Charlie, he was barely a child himself. I tried to support him as best I could but am not sure I gave him enough help as he struggled with his new role. It was another reminder that many of us, whatever our age, struggle to be a parent. But love usually finds a way. I am gushing with pride to know that, as a family we are now all so close to Davie. Charlie has grown into a great man, a great dad and is a steady role model for Davie. Just like his own dad, Charlie loves, provides and is a great protector. But he is an even better parent than me and Derek!

Then a few incidents happened that made me start to feel unsafe in Croydon, including being burgled a couple of times. One night, Billy was glassed in a pub. I saw the footage of what happened and it sickened me. As Billy entered the pub, this guy walked straight up to him and smashed Billy in the face with a pint glass. There was no conversation, nothing. Billy went straight down. It was horrendous. The case went to court and I was a witness. We didn't know it at the time but the guy already had a record for smashing bottles into people's faces. He was part of a vicious family who were notorious for being violent. I went to each court case and I managed to remain calm, even though I was sitting among this family, knowing how violent they were. One of them tried to warn me off, through Charlie, advising him that I may want to think again before testifying. Even my brother Jim questioned whether I should go ahead with the case as he had received a phone call from someone in prison, telling him to warn me off. I did question myself and wondered if I should back down on this occasion, even though every fibre of my being always wants to fight injustice. I couldn't have lived with myself if my principles put my boys at risk. But then, I couldn't have lived with myself if I didn't stand up to those bastards. This was my son who had been hurt, he'd been lucky not to lose his eye and what was to stop this maniac glassing someone else, what if someone else's son was killed? No, I had to do what I knew was right and I refused to be intimidated. He was found guilty and given a four year sentence. His family went mental when they walked out of the court, swearing and carrying on. It was very scary but it was all worth it: justice had been served.

It wasn't too long before I was once again witness in a violent crime case. I had gone to the pub with Sonia and another friend and we were at the bar when, out of nowhere the barmaid started picking a fight with my friend.

"I know your fucking husband," she said. My friend, who was the smallest out of the three of us, didn't know what this barmaid was talking about. For once, I was completely sober and I could feel the atmosphere in the pub darken. At that point, I didn't know that the barmaid's family was also in the pub, I just knew that we had to go, quickly.

"Get your keys," I said quietly to my friend. But it was too late, the pub doors were locked and my friend was set upon by a whole group of people. The violence was so extreme, so excessive and so random, I had never seen anything like it. This crowd were punching my friend and she was on the floor being kicked in the head as I tried to get her up, while Sonia was at the door screaming for them to let us out. After about 10 minutes they lifted her up on to a table and carried on attacking her. It was so appalling, like witnessing someone being murdered. Eventually, a man picked up our friend and put her slight, limp body into a car. We drove in silence, thinking she may be dead. When we got to our house Derek called an ambulance and the police.

It was such an awful thing to have witnessed and I was

in so much shock that I had a couple of months of therapy to work through it. I also went to Thailand with my brother Jeff and my mum, I think she paid for the ticket. Once again, my mum – the woman who was no stranger to violence – acted as my rescuer. We had a nice holiday but it was clear to me that Fay was already plotting to try and get Delaine back under her control. By this time Delaine had been out of the family for a while, and Fay was trying to pull her back in. Both Jeff and I knew that the fallout from that would be that one of the rest of us would get kicked out. We both told her to leave it and let Delaine make her own life decisions.

By the time the court case came up I was in good shape, thanks to the counselling and my holiday. It wasn't nice in court but it proved to be a traumatic experience for Sonia, who hadn't really processed what had happened, the horror of it. We had to watch the stomach-turning footage and I think the whole thing triggered Sonia. I witnessed her suffer from the fallout for a couple of years. I'm pleased to say she's fine now and her life is good. Again, this was a powerful reminder that our body and brain keeps note and has to create an outlet for terror. I feel this shared experience of fear changed us both for a while and created a close bond between us that words could not explain. I think she felt it, too. I often wondered if that's what militaries feel about their comrades after sharing terrifying experiences, a bond of deep trust and kinship.

As for the eight or so perpetrators of that disgusting attack, some of them received a conditional discharge and not one of them served time for their crime. Justice was not served this time.

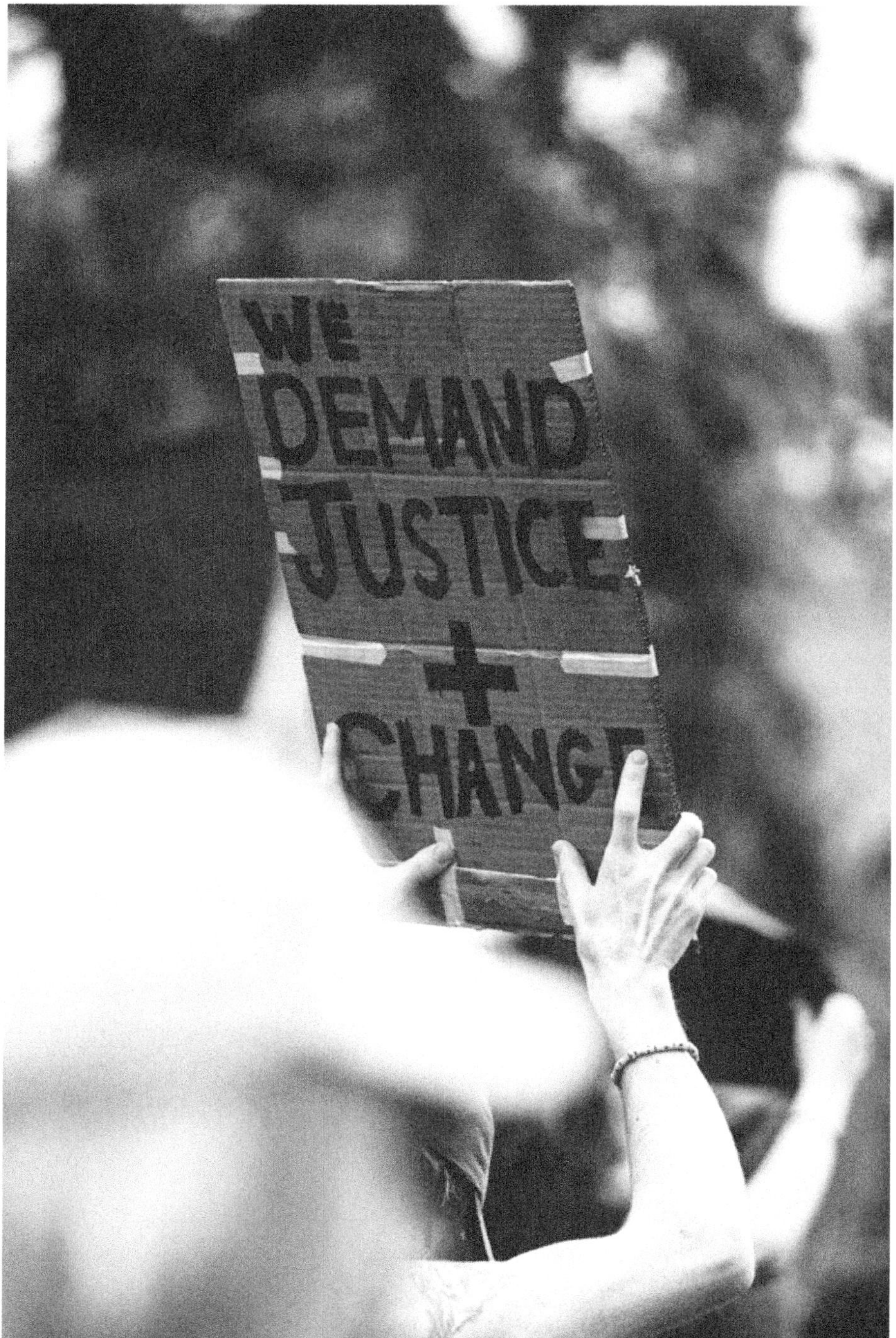
WE
DEMAND
JUSTICE
+
CHANGE

12

NEW START

Soundtrack: Amy Winehouse, Duffy, Adele, Jess Glynne, Rudimentals, Florence and the Machine, Rihanna

Viv is barely recognisable, she looks so frail and old. But she still has that same twinkle in her eye. "Come on, then," she says, gesturing towards a pile of underwear on the table. "Knickers on heads everyone!"

Viv was only in her 60s when she was diagnosed with liver failure. I hadn't seen her for a while and then, when I heard about her illness, I phoned her regularly and she sounded exactly the same. So I wasn't prepared for the first time I met her again and I couldn't hide my shock to see her looking so thin and old. I started spending as much time with her as I could and was pleased to see the old Viv was still there. During her last Christmas with us, she arranged a little drinks party. She was very poorly as this point and couldn't drink herself, but made sure there was plenty for us. She would take a little sip every now and then to make it look as though she was joining in. I think she was coughing up blood in the toilet, but you would never have known. She was so incredibly brave and, as always, generous. She most probably knew it was her last Christmas and she had bought us all wine and chocolates, made sure we all had a wonderful time. When I got home I just cried and cried. Over the years we had shared so many lovely times, so many laughs, so many wonderful conversations. She was such a good friend and a great human being.

There were around 400 people at her funeral, she was so loved. Her husband, Jim, is like an Irish Derek, so gentle and kind, and all her kids are amazing. The family asked me to write a few words about Viv for the funeral. What an honour! I don't know if they realise how much they all mean to me. I hope Viv knew how much I valued her.

By this time I had a new job. In 2009 I decided to leave RASASC (now called South London Rape Crisis). I have so much respect for that organisation and the women who work there. They make a difference and not just on ground level: they are in Government, they sit on Scotland Yard panels, they are challenging the Ministry of Justice. Their training and knowledge is second to none and the ten years I spent there changed me profoundly. But after a decade of working and studying, I was feeling a little burned out and decided to take six months off to rest and recharge. It had taken me many years to realise that I needed – and deserved – to take care of myself properly. Then I started working for Women's Aid as a residential service officer, supporting women who are fleeing the most appalling domestic violence. It's curious how I was always attracted to jobs that overlapped with my own story.

In 2011, I took some more time out and I spent a month in Thailand on my own. It was amazing: for once I wasn't a mother, wife or daughter, I was just me. I wasn't entirely on my own because my niece Lainey was out there, which was like a safety net for me. I got a little apartment and hired a car and I would drive around listening to music, especially Rihanna. It was so liberating. I would go and sit in buddhist temples, soaking up the serenity. I talked to lots of people and was in awe of everyone's humility. Derek came to stay for the last couple of weeks and we had a fantastic time.

One night, we were sitting in a bar that had a TV and there was a surreal moment when I said to Derek, "There seem to be an awful lot of British police on that telly." And I kept watching. "That's where we live!" I said, as pictures of Croydon came on the screen. It was chaos, people were running around rioting and buses were on fire. "Shit, my kids!" I cried. When I phoned home, they were both safely inside – Billy was busy making cups of tea for all the grannies!

My trip to Thailand gave me a new lease of life, it was time to turn a new page. In 2004 we had bought a field in Lingfield, Surrey and we spent weekends camping there with the boys. My brother Jim and family would join us caravanning some weekends, which was perfect. It was so beautiful there and provided the breath of fresh air we needed as a family. It was my safe place. So when we decided to sell our house in Croydon and escape the city for good, we moved to Lingfield. Derek had been working as an HGV fitter in Lingfield for the last decade, so now at last he was nearer to work. Although I knew it was time for us to leave the estate we'd called home for 17 years, it was not without some sadness. We had enjoyed some happy family times in that house and I had watched my sons grow into young men there. It was a very sociable home and we'd had lots of fun there. We'd had a bird flu party, Kate and William wedding party, Elvis party, England football match parties – any excuse for a party!

Moving house also meant moving away from my cousin Donna, who also lived on the estate. We were always in and out of each other's homes as our children grew up together. We would go clubbing and pubbing and have many days out with a carful of our children having fun – being normal. We laughed together and supported each other like sisters. She was my best friend, one of the few people I trusted fully and without her by my side my journey would have been a lonely place. Even though Derek is wonderful, there is a unique bond between women that is essential to the soul and its healing. I love Donna with all my heart and her wonderful children. After all those years on the estate, I knew it was going to be strange not to have Donna living just a road away from me. But I also knew it was time.

Initially the plan had been to build a house on our field, which was a lovely dream but not very realistic. Instead we bought a fantastic maisonette in Lingfield village and we loved our idyllic new home, even when it was full of high-vis jackets, muddy boots and lorry batteries.

The boys had grown into wonderful young men. I had always drummed it into them: you have two choices when you live where we live, you either learn and work hard or you deal drugs. Thank goodness they both chose hard work. Charlie didn't sit any exams, but instead he walked around for hours and hours asking if there were any mechanic apprenticeships going. He ended up being offered two, one for cars and one for lorries, which was absolutely amazing as they are really hard to come by. Charlie chose lorries because he already knew there was more money to be earned there and he was right. He now has his own thriving lorry business. Billy took his Class 1 HGV licence as soon as he could and from a young age was driving these huge articulated lorries. I take my hat off to both of them, they have done so well through their own hard graft. I am such a proud mum. They both have their own places now but over the years have stayed at our flat for various reasons and that's when we would be overrun with high-vis jackets and petrol-related items!

In 2012 I began a whole new adventure. I was becoming increasingly frustrated with the system of supporting women with violence because they were coming into the refuge and then leaving again without having learned anything about domestic abuse. So they were vulnerable to it all over again. I realised there was something missing, that we needed to provide women with some tools to protect themselves. I heard about some fantastic work and got talking to Pat Craven, a probation officer who created the Freedom Programme, which educates women about the tactics of perpetrators. I was fascinated and got Derek to drive me to Newcastle to do a three-day course about the programme. Afterwards, I thought, *I need to leave my job.*

So I did. I handed in my notice at Women's Aid and set up my own business, which I called Freedom Together. I knew I was taking a huge risk but I also knew I was in a good place to do this, because I had been working in this field for 12 years and had built up a lot of contacts. I had a waiting list from day one.

My vision was that I would start running education programmes for women. I wanted to empower and protect women and children by giving them as much knowledge as possible. It was teaching women to have the resilience and courage to move forward, to have a voice and speak about their trauma. Taking the Freedom Programme as the core, I developed a programme that also incorporated my own knowledge and experience. My first idea was that women who were not yet high risk would walk in, but it didn't work like that. I was getting social care referrals from everywhere, including GPs and safeguarding leads in schools. I never had a chance to open it up to anyone else because I was always full. I sought out funding and partnershipped with everyone I could so that I could offer the workshops to women for free.

I worked with each group for three months. My former Women's Aid boss Pauline helped me deliver groupwork and I was privileged to work with other amazing women who were expert in working with kids and families. I always tried to create the sort of environment that I would want to walk into. I held courses right across Croydon and tried to find places that felt safe. I liked using children's centres because they are always secure, warm and friendly. Before the group arrived, I would prepare the room so that it was sensuous and inviting. I sprayed lovely fragrances and always had music playing as they walked in, just to break any nervous silence and calm nerves. Then I provided cakes, as well as lots of lovely lotions for them to use. In my funding applications, I would always be asked why are you buying hand creams, is this essential? And I would say, 'Oh yes it absolutely is.' I tried to create a little pampering parlour, knowing that there would be some very hard, very brave, very difficult work going on in these group sessions. It was sensitive work but I didn't hold back or skirt around things, I told the truth even when it was uncomfortable and I really went to those dark places with them.

I pushed hard for funding so that I could also start doing these courses for 13- to 21-year-olds. These were girls at risk, with key workers, girls like me. These girls really touched me because I could see myself in them. Meetings were held to discuss adapting what I did, to make it more suitable for their younger age, but I said no, we do it full on. I recruited the girls by asking if they wanted to learn about gang violence, perpetrators and abuse. I was very boundaried with them and said they had to commit to the full three months and not mess me about and, amazingly, they all came!

Then in between my own programme, I was still working for Rape Crisis, delivering courses on consent and rape to pupil referral units with their wonderful team. These were girls and boys who were at risk of being excluded from school, they were on their last chance. It was challenging and chaotic working with these units but I loved it. While delivering the Freedom Together projects to young girls, the lippiest ones, the girls originally most hostile, would so often be the ones who would be crying at the end of the course, they'd totally softened and wanted to learn as much as possible.

I think the main thing I've always wanted to teach these women and girls is that they have a voice. I cannot say it enough. Perpetrators put out their fire and silence them. At the beginning of a session, when we were introducing ourselves I would say you don't have to speak until you want to, until you feel OK. It was a way of giving them back the power that had been taken from them. Some had been so depleted that they didn't even know what their favourite colour was, or their favourite food. It was about enabling them to see that they had lost something precious in themselves, or maybe they never had it if they had suffered child abuse. I wanted to enable them to feel that they were wonderful, valuable people in the world: they weren't bad mums or shit people, they were not simply a label – drug addict or shoplifter – they were people who have suffered terrible trauma at the hands of another. The thing I find myself saying time and again is, 'You are not bad and you're not crazy, you have had a normal response to someone else's abnormal behaviour.'

I have received so many cards from women thanking me for changing their lives, which is so wonderful. At first, I had to battle with my familiar imposter syndrome and my mum's voice saying, 'Who do you think you are?' Now I think, yes I have made a difference and I can feel proud of the work I've done. Most recently I had an email from a woman who said, 'Lou, you've given me the voice.' She told me that, because of what I'd taught her, she was able to see that her child was being abused by the dad and now she was fighting in court to protect her infant. 'I am having interviews to stop the contact between them and my child has disclosed to me,' she wrote. 'And I have been able to calmly deal with it, even though I am dying inside.' It made me cry because, to keep a child safe, that is worth everything.

These women have taught me so many lessons, too. I have met women who have been sectioned, written off, who cannot speak, who have sold their bodies, lost themselves to drugs, been obliterated by their abuser, lost their sight, their children, their mobility, their sanity. They have been through some horrendous things and I applaud them for their courage. It has been a complete privilege to work with these beautiful women.

Sometimes you have to be your own hero.

13

FACING THE STORM

Soundtrack: Barbra Streisand, The Carpenters, Jess Glynne – 'Take Me Home'

At the bottom of the piece of paper, I draw a tiny matchstick girl. She is crying and has her eyes cast down to the floor. Above her looms a huge face, so big it fills the whole sheet of paper. The mouth on this face is screaming swear words at the matchstick girl. This is what I draw when my therapist asks me to create a picture of me and my mum.

Fay's physical attacks had stopped when I was 16, the day after I left school, but there are more subtle ways to abuse your children – and your children's children. In 2014 Fay turned her attentions to Delaine's daughter Lainey and tried to control her to such an extent that she made my niece ill. Fay tried to turn the family against my niece but I wasn't having any part in Fay's hate campaign and told her so. My niece, who is a beautiful soul, withdrew from the family and no longer trusts us, which causes me huge sadness. She wasn't to know that many of us hated what Fay did and never condoned her punishing behaviour. Fay was starting to remind me of the cruel, bullying woman I had witnessed first hand and I was now witnessing her damaging, controlling behaviour in the next generation.

After causing this terrible rift in the family, Fay had a new project. She summoned me, my sister Delaine, brother Jeff and even my sons for a meeting at her house in Herne Bay. My other brother Jim was out of the family at this time – it was his turn. She sent us all a text telling us she had serious news but not to contact her before we met up in a week's time. I was really worried, imagining the worst, that either Fay or George was very sick. In the end I texted her and said, 'Mum let me phone you just to know that you are OK.' She refused to answer my calls and she sent me an angry text back that said, 'For once in your life will you just leave it and do as I say. Wait until the weekend.'

That phrase 'For once in your life' triggered me. I had heard it from her so many times at the start of a physical or verbal attack: 'For once in your f***ing life do as you're f***ing told,' slap, 'you stupid –', *slap, punch, whack*. So when I heard it then, it told me she was lying. My sons were really worried about Fay's 'serious' news and were going to take time off work to come with us. I told them not to, that if it was anything serious I promised I'd let them know straight away. I couldn't be sure that she was going to lie to us, what if it were true this time? Surely even Fay wouldn't mess with her grandsons' heads? But I couldn't get rid of my suspicions, because it wouldn't be the first time she had gaslighted us. On the way to Fay's a week later, I spoke to my brother Jeff and we both agreed the news would most likely be that Fay or George was dying and that she would most likely be lying. But I resolved to hear her out.

When we got to my mum's she was all bubbly and smiley and sat us down. We had all been feeling upset, anxious, worried and angry all week.

"Where do I start, George?" she asked, making the most of our rapt attention. "Is it you or Dad?" I asked bluntly. Then she said she didn't want to upset anyone but she'd made her bucket list and when she started losing her hair she was going to wear a blonde wig. Then she joked about how funny this would be. It was horrendous, particularly since I had quite recently lost a dear friend. I asked her what kind of cancer she had and she said throat. I started asking her questions about it and it just wasn't adding up. I absolutely knew she was lying. Fay had obviously forgotten she'd told me she had cancer ten years earlier and this story didn't follow up on her previous one. I asked her when she had had the tests and what she was diagnosed with. She said, "I haven't had the tests yet, but the doctor is 99 per cent sure it's throat cancer."

"So you haven't been diagnosed yet?" I asked.

At this point Fay exploded. "You never f***ing listen!

You can't even let me die in peace – how I want to!" I was shaking with anger inside, but didn't want to lose it, or be aggressive. Jeff left the room and Delaine couldn't look at her. I told Fay that what she was doing was abusive, but she replied that none of us ever supported her. She even took Delaine and I upstairs to pick which bits of her jewellery we wanted, as keepsakes.

Then, just a day or two later she texted with the miraculous news: 'Yipee, I got the test results back, I'm fine!' She may not have had cancer but she was certainly sick.

"I can't do this anymore," I told her. "It's shocking what you're doing to us." Predictably, Fay exploded and turned it around so that it was my fault. I had finally had enough of Fay's emotional control, which was so subtle and so manipulative that it was hard to recognise as abuse. I challenged her behaviour in texts and emails, I could no longer talk to her. This is the same woman who I would see so often sitting on her couch, cigarette in hand, counselling other people about their relationships. Her friends thought that we, her children, were disgusting in our behaviour towards her. I suppose they, too, were unwitting victims of her manipulative abuse.

It is only the victims who see a full 360-degree view of the personality of their abuser. Others outside the abuse will only have access to what a perpetrator will allow you to see. The saying, 'You never know what goes on behind closed doors' is true. A victim once told me that all the kids in her area loved her dad and wanted to have a dad like hers. He would play football with the kids outside and invite them all in, all friendly and joking. What they did not see was the broken jaw he gave her mum in his rages when the door was closed.

As my relationship with my mum now began a steady decline, we were introduced to a new member of the family when George's long-lost son Andy turned up. Now aged 49, Andy had been adopted as a baby and George never knew about him. He got in touch through Facebook and wanted to meet us, so we gave our best impression of being a united family and met with Andy and his wife and kids. Incredibly, it turned out that for all those years he had been living really close by. I didn't want to build too close a relationship with Andy because I knew that my relationship with Fay and George was fading. But I did get chatting with Andy's partner, Kelly. She said she thought Fay was quite a character and she told me that Fay had been laughing about how fiery she'd been and about what she'd been like as a mum. I couldn't believe my ears. Fay was boasting and laughing, laughing about the fact that she was so violent and how she would fight George and how hard a mother she was. Kelly had no idea the conversation was reminding me how Fay had beaten me black and blue, terrorised and bullied me and made me feel that I was a worthless nobody. No, there was absolutely nothing funny about my childhood. This was the final straw.

While I remained distant from Fay, she still tried to exert some control over me via my biggest vulnerability – my sons. Having started my therapy, I was even more acutely aware of Fay's controlling behaviour and I sensed that she was trying to turn my boys against me. This thought was in my mind when Derek and I went on holiday to Malta and when we came back I texted my sons and told them that if their nan had been in touch while I was away, I wanted them to know that I was well and happy and they should ask me if they wanted to know anything. Within minutes they had both contacted me and I was absolutely right. Fay had been in touch with them to say that I needed looking after, that I was having a bad time and wasn't feeling right. Neither Billy nor Charlie was having any of it, in fact Charlie had a row with Fay over it because she kept going on at him to look after me. I'm glad to say that my sons have minds of their own and the voice I never had. They spoke up, telling her I was perfectly fine and enjoying a lovely holiday with their dad. This latest ploy from my mum broke me all over again, she was so toxic, so relentless and so subtle in her control. This is called gaslighting.

But here's yet another complicated aspect of abuse. You miss your abuser when you are separated from them. I have seen women in refuges crying, ashamed to tell anyone they miss their abusers. Once separated from the person who is hurting them, they feel as though they have lost themselves. This is hardly surprising given that abusers isolate you, so that all you have is them, they are thieves who steal your independence, your self-esteem.

We needed to confront Fay to let her know that we were not going to tolerate her appalling behaviour any longer. So I sent a message asking if Jeff, Delaine and myself could meet with her and George to discuss the future and how we wanted it to be for our family. I had been so angry at the time she told us about the cancer, but now the three of us just wanted to move forward. This wasn't about confrontation or hostility, I reassured her, but finding a way to put an end to the hurt and the games so that we could all move on. I hoped this would be well received, but my request wasn't even acknowledged until my birthday, when I received an email from Fay that killed any hope of peaceful, adult conversation. She said that she and George were agreed that there was no case to answer, nothing to talk about and she didn't expect to hear from me ever again.

When I read her email I was knocked sideways. But I had to try and hold myself together because my sons and their girlfriends had organised a lovely birthday meal for me. I didn't know that the rest of my family and their kids were also going to be there. I was overwhelmed that they had all organised such a lovely surprise for me, but I had to hold back my tears because I didn't want my anger at Fay to come out, too. She wasn't going to spoil this wonderful evening that had been arranged with such loving kindness. But I knew there was no coming back from this with Fay.

She was never ever going to behave like an adult and take any responsibility for her actions. And as long as she refused to do this, she would continue to damage us. I decided to cut all contact with her and I would have to break away from George, too, because they came as a package.

And then, predictably, she started sending me lovely messages on my birthday, at Christmas. She would send the boys home with flowers for me, or beautifully wrapped gifts. I knew exactly what she was doing, she was trying to control my responses. That's the double-sided confusion of domestic abuse: perpetrators punch with one hand and offer beautiful gifts with the other. Some women experience this 'love bombing' from abusive partners. The boys didn't understand what she was up to and couldn't see why I threw away her gifts. "She's just being nice," they said. But I knew different.

Throughout our lives, we four siblings – me, Jim, Delaine and Jeff – were rarely all together, one of us was always left out. But now we decided that we were not going to continue to let her fragment us. We made a pact to always stay together, to respect each other's differences, to keep in touch and be nice to one another. We decided to stand together always. This was a very meaningful place to reach, as we each have our own awful stories around adults who did nothing to protect us. And we were all agreed that we'd had enough of all the hurt we had experienced. We have all dipped in and out of Fay and George's lives, just glad to be the ones being loved rather than excluded.

I went through the process of grieving the loss of the mother I yearned for and a man I had loved as a father. I was beginning to feel exhausted and burned out and wondered if I needed to give up work. I recognised I was suffering symptoms of trauma and attributed it to work burnout, vicarious trauma. My fantastic clinical supervisor Shirani, who had supported me in my work since my days in Rape Crisis, suggested that I go back into therapy and I knew that this was what I needed. I think it was clearer to her that it was the trauma of my mother's continuous gaslighting rather than my career that was wringing me out. In my mind, if I was ever going to free myself from the tyranny of trauma I had to face up to it, not just for me but also for the women I worked with. I found the very best therapist, called Sarah, and with her expertise I started to unlock those emotions and memories.

This was very intense therapy indeed, including some years of trauma therapy and nearly all of it focused on my mum's abuse. This challenging work uncovered just how lonely and scared I had been throughout my younger years and it also brought back some body memories. As a young girl I remember going to school after severe emotional and physical assaults. At the time I saw all the marks and the bruises and I knew it was awful but I don't remember feeling anything at all. This is dissociation, I had disconnected from my abuse. Now it was all surfacing. This is called feeling and healing, I was connecting in body and mind.

The intense brain-spotting trauma work also revealed to me the pre-verbal abuse that Tony had inflicted on me as a baby. These were things I always knew had happened, but I was unable to connect the words to feelings. Therapy was absolutely harrowing and it was all so raw. Once I really started to safely process all those stored-up emotions and all that physical pain, I had nowhere to hide. I had to just sit with all those feelings welling up inside me. This mainly happened at weekends. I functioned fine at work, but then at weekends it was as though my brain knew it was OK to let go. I would regress into a vulnerable, distressed, lonely little girl and sometimes it felt unbearable. The healing felt more like dying as I processed a lifetime of stored raw emotions. But I needed to do this. I sat in my trauma and I cried a lot and, as always calmed myself with music. 'Why Worry' by Dire Straits was a song that really soothed my heart after I had a flashback or regressed into that vulnerable, traumatised state. Sung by Geordies, it's a song that reminds me of Derek, of being held in his strong, loving arms and feeling so close to him. My brother Jeff also held me through this terrible time, often talking to me daily, helping me laugh and cry, giving me encouragement. He knew my pain. Safe people at these times are like paramedics, lifesavers. Jeff is a good man.

I've always been honest with my sons and during this time I told them, "I'm not feeling right, I've gone back to counselling and I'm dealing with some stuff, so just bear with me." They were accepting and amazing. What wonderful men they have become, just like their dad. Derek, as always, just listened to me, he understood that I needed to get upset in order to recover. It was just waves and waves of old abuse and it got so bad that I said to him at one point, "I don't think I can make it." He said, "You can." I knew I had reached a place where I felt I could no longer cope. I just wanted the pain and memories to end. I had suicidal thoughts. The strong urges to binge away my pain were fierce. I thought of drink, heroin, overdosing, hanging, cutting myself, running away from my life. I yearned to walk away from all my responsibilities and disappear onto the streets, to drink and just leave everything behind. I came to understand that this was my younger traumatised child. In my recovery I had regressed, finally connecting to feelings from my past. This was the disturbed child in a woman's body. It was so confusing and distressing, I often could not talk but I was healing with each day that passed.

One of the things that kept me going was our beautiful field. We would go there at weekends and sometimes I would be in a terrible state. We didn't speak and I would just plough up ground and cut grass and mend things. And I would look at nature and draw and listen to music, always music. It was my saviour.

While the therapy was slowly healing my trauma, I started taking better care of myself. I stopped overeating and gave up alcohol – for good. After all those years of binge drinking, alcohol suddenly felt like poison to me, perhaps because I knew I now had to experience my feelings instead of numbing them. And actually it feels much more like the real me to be sitting in a corner drinking tea, rather than being the drunken life and soul of the party. I connected to my artistic side, too. I had always been good at drawing at school and I discovered I was still good at it.

I did a lot of research on trauma, because I wanted to use everything I was learning in my therapy to help traumatised women in my own sessions. I understood that you need to get your body working with your mind, to get it connected. Singing, I discovered, is a fantastic way to release trauma because it connects you to your breathing and grounds you. I started joining choirs and found the most amazing one called Singing Mamas Choir. Led by a woman called Kate, this community choir was inclusive, wholesome and nurturing and I loved it. The first time I went I was so delighted to see children there, too. Toddlers and babies were not being screamed at to shut up, but were free to sit or toddle around, soaking up all of this joy. Those beautiful women just held you safe among them and singing with them was such an uplifting experience. Somewhere within me was the little girl who just yearned for consistent love without the games, the emotional distress. I wanted to be those children who, in the choir, were being bathed in gentle song and tenderness.

I wanted to share this with the women who came to Freedom Together, so I started offering creative workshops called Free 2 B projects, which included yoga, belly dancing, fit dance and singing. I asked the Singing Mamas to lead some sessions and it was amazing to see these traumatised women – many of whom would never have joined a choir – find their voices. They cried, they laughed and I felt really touched to just stand back and listen to them singing together, to watch them being so joyful, so empowered. Another highlight for me were the jiggling tums and belly laughs at the belly dancing workshops as confidence grew and inhibitions melted away.

I finally accepted that Fay's presence in my life was toxic, that I could only be happy and healthy if I cut her out of it, I felt bereft. For about a year, I spent a lot of time soothing my sadness by listening to Barbra Streisand and the Carpenters as I drove in my car. I was grieving for Fay. I mourned the loss of her in my life, but I mainly grieved for the parents I never had in Fay and George, the parents I always yearned for.

when you
come out of
the storm
you won't
be the same
person who
walked in.
that's what
this storm is
all about.

14

THE JOURNEY CONTINUES

Soundtrack: *Ralph McTell – 'Streets of London', Fleetwood Mac – 'Landslide', Stormzy – 'Blinded By Your Grace'*

I look up at the stage and see those awesome women, my fellow speakers. Then I see my name on a huge screen, describing me as a specialist in domestic abuse. I am triggered. I shrink back, I am totally lost, I can't speak, my voice has gone, I want to cry and I am shaking. I try to fight my brain but it is a losing battle. I am totally disconnected from everyone in the room, I can't hear what anyone is saying, I am completely helpless. Soon it will be my turn to stand on that stage and speak. What am I going to do?

A couple of years ago I was asked to be a guest speaker at a conference about violence against women and girls. It was a big event, in the town hall, with members of the Government and high-ranking police officers attending. I knew it was a great forum to talk about domestic abuse and the long-term effects. The other speakers included Payzee Mahmod, sister of Banaz, the young woman killed by her father in an honour-based killing and another courageous woman who'd been a child bride. I was in awe of these amazing women who had been through so much and here I was, sharing the stage with them in front of all these important people. That thought was enough to trigger me. I went into full imposter syndrome and heard that dark voice – my mother's – saying, 'Who the hell do you think you are?'

At that moment I knew I needed to take care of myself. Sitting in the audience I saw some women I'd worked with and I said, "Budge up, let me sit with you – don't ask." I held myself together until my name was called. Despite my fear, I managed to get myself up on stage. I asked them to turn off the microphone because I couldn't bear to hear my voice amplified. And I told everyone what had just happened to me, how I had been triggered.

'I can't speak, can't get my thoughts together because this is the realistic truth of it," I explained. "I am a professional but I am also a survivor, a victim of abuse and it never goes away. So I could stand here and pretend I'm OK but I'm not going to. This is trauma." I told them that I may have to step down from the stage at any point and that, if I did, I hoped they would understand. Then I was able to give my talk and explain that there was no quick fix, that recovery from domestic and sexual violence is a slow process and we need to work with women long term. I was exhausted afterwards but proud of myself that I had managed to get through it.

Despite how far I have travelled now in my healing, I can still be triggered at any time. This is when the emotional part of my brain completely overrides the rational part, I cannot see or think clearly and I dissociate. Then there's the constant threat of imposter syndrome, which makes it hard for me to feel I deserve any recognition or praise for my achievements. Even when I started writing this book, there was that nasty niggling little voice asking me who I thought I was to be writing a book? But I am getting better at ignoring that voice and do sometimes feel proud of myself.

One of those moments happened recently when I managed to actually sing – live and solo – in front of an online audience of hundreds. During the Covid pandemic, the Singing Mamas have been doing online choirs and they asked me if I would teach a song to everyone. I chose Ralph McTell's 'Streets of London' because of the lyrics: it's saying to people, open your eyes and see what's going on out there, take notice, be loving, be kind. The song was so deeply linked to my life, reminding me of myself as a teenager, of all the women I work with who are fleeing domestic abuse, carrying their life in a plastic bag. Ralph McTell has close links to Croydon so that was another good reason for choosing it. I barely slept the night before and was a bag of nerves on the day, but I did it. And I loved it!

The photo of me in this book, holding up the note

that says 'We have a voice' was taken that day. It's such a beautiful message for all those who have survived domestic abuse or any form of violence: we can speak out, we can sing with joy together. And, for me, that image represents such a milestone in my life, it's me rising from the ashes like a phoenix, of feeling the fear and doing it anyway. My singing may not have been quite so poetic, but you can't have everything!

I have also reached a significant moment in my career because I am stepping away from Freedom Together. I am a little exhausted from the uphill struggle to find funding amid ever-decreasing resources, and disillusioned by a legal system that victim shames, that is increasingly giving perpetrators custody of children, and that simply does not understand trauma. I feel that I need a rest and also to create some time for me. I will never stop supporting those women and children, never stop holding the hope for them that things can change and helping to empower them to gain belief in themselves. And I will never stop fighting for the justice that these women and children see so rarely. I am still going to work within the field of domestic and sexual violence for a little while longer, raising awareness among particular communities and I will also be delivering training for South London Rape Crisis. It is always an honour to work with this outstanding organisation and join the tribe that I hold in such high esteem. I also plan to offer retreats for frontline staff working with domestic and sexual abuse, education and health, as well as wellbeing workshops for all women.

There is more need than ever for us to talk about domestic violence towards women and children. During the coronavirus pandemic, soaring rates of domestic abuse and child sexual abuse have brought demand for our workshops. Abuse thrives on silence and I will never stop encouraging women to have a voice. Now that I have found mine, I am going to use it all my life. My family wanted me to remain silent, just as they did, about the sexual abuse I suffered at the hands of a trusted family member. There will be some family members who do not understand why I wanted to write this book. They want to maintain the fiction that everything is fine, they want to keep those dark secrets, secrets that will continue to harm future generations if they stay buried.

We are built to survive; we are also built to thrive. I feel the body will keep nudging us to acknowledge our pain so that we open the door to recovery, but many, like me, will mask it with pain relief. We are not robots, we are sensitive, fragile beings and if we are harmed we hold a wave of feelings and madness that is aching to be heard. When you silence someone by suggesting they should not feel or be a certain way, it keeps their wounds open.

This book is an honest reflection of my story, taken from my memories of childhood into my current life. It is a story that has harmed me for far too long because it remained unspoken. The fact is, my mum's family know a generation of violent and aggressive controlling parents and partners, but they would rather we maintain the façade that we all lived happily ever after. Some would rather not acknowledge the children who witnessed the abuse and refuse to believe that they, too, were victims. Many of my cousins have nice homes, jobs and are sociable people, however most have been impacted greatly by their exposure to unhealthy, abnormal behaviour. Most of my family's generation, if not all, have suffered with their mental health at some point in our lives: feeling suicidal, depressed, self-harming, with low self-esteem and always striving to feel good enough. Many of us kept silent because no one wants to speak the truth of the harm that plagued our homes. I have family who I love dearly but who still show photos of Tony, totally in denial of the harm he has caused. Keeping silent becomes toxic in families and can slowly poison us.

My mother will never acknowledge what she has done, nor take responsibility for it. I am not writing this book to demonise her. It wasn't all bad – she bought me my first car, we shared some nice family holidays and Christmases – and I know she is a very damaged person who has suffered her own abuse. She didn't take her own journey of recovery, so she projected all her hate and rage onto her children and she passed the trauma to another generation. Like many, she chooses not to talk openly, not acknowledge the hurt. I don't hate her, I just know that I cannot have good mental health if she is in my life. As for Tony, words cannot express what he took from me and I am unable to feel free in my body still. Thank goodness I had all the love and kindness I needed in my marriage. Without it I don't think I would still be here.

I am now very aware how historical trauma can be passed down through generations. I can't believe that my trauma didn't affect my boys in some way. I think about all the times I was unable to rest or make my brain stay calm, all those years of stealing from shops while they sat in their buggies, of overspending, overeating, overeverything! In my disconnected state, did I make them feel as if they had upset me, or that I was distant? It took me 29 years to realise how my own internal struggles could become theirs, but all is not lost. I know from my own recovery that having a voice is the pathway to healing. So if ever I have made them feel alone or unloved they can share it with me, it can be named and talked about. I want my sons to know that I attach shame to my mothering, but my love for them has allowed me to love myself enough to want change. My grandson Davie has my full connection and sees a much more peaceful adult than my young sons ever did.

This book is the truth of my life. I wrote it for me, for my sons and Derek, and for any survivor who recognises a part of herself in my story. To all those women I would say, we are not mad, we are traumatised. We have been exposed to things that no one should experience. Trauma is a normal reaction to the experience of shock and terror. So be kind and gentle to yourselves, give yourselves all those things you've never received from others. And recognise that it's not you who's abnormal, it's those perpetrators who've done it to you.

To everyone who is reading this book I would also say, listen to children and believe them. They do not lie, they do not make up abuse. Once you disbelieve one child, you have silenced another ten for that perpetrator. If you stand by and do nothing, you have also silenced that child. CHILDREN DO NOT LIE ABOUT ABUSE. It's time we listened to them.

If we all take responsibility for our behaviour towards children, their mental health would be significantly improved, as everything we do impacts on a child's development. Our first three years is by far the most important in our brain's development. A baby's brain is creating 3,000 new cells each second, absorbing all its environment like a sponge. So, if a baby is exposed to anger, fear, threat or neglect, they are building a complex hard drive from which they grow, or freeze and crash – just as I did on several occasions. You may not outwardly see the damage being caused, as not all children act out, but it can corrode the child's ability to value and love themselves. We are not computers, we are living, breathing human beings: recovery from abuse can take years. What we need from the start is love, nurturing, kindness, patience, and compassion.

If you have dismissed a disclosure from a close friend or family member because it was too difficult to believe, you have helped to silence the voice of the victim. I have heard countless accounts of women and children disclosing abuse, domestic and sexual violence by someone they know, and the response from family is to stay quiet, disbelieve, minimise the abuse, or worst of all, vilify the victim. It is important we all recognise that perpetrators rarely show who they really are, otherwise they would all be in jail. The Tonys of this world present themselves as kind, funny, even a hero in their community. It is a well-known fact that sexual predators often have a charitable side, investing time in good causes whilst targeting their victims. Jimmy Savile, for example, raised over £35 million for charitable causes. Many of his victims were dismissed and called liars!

Fortunately, I have lived to tell you that you can get through this. Your journey may be slow and need many attempts, kindness and support, but there will come a time when you can begin to recover. Recovery is not forgetting it happened or shutting it out, it is being brave, being vulnerable and being heard. I hope my story will encourage others to believe that we can heal, we can find our voice. I am the living proof that you can. The journey is an ongoing process. Even now, in my safe, happy home, there are still times when those buried feelings surface and I regress into that terrified little girl who feels she doesn't deserve love or even life itself. But now I understand what's happening and have the tools to look after myself. The party girl now soothes herself with tea, singing and gardening!

There have been times, in my trauma, when I feared that suicide was a possibility. But now something has shifted in me and I want to reassure my boys that I'm not going anywhere, I intend to be a wobbly old mum and granny. I love my life and see a bright future. I will never forget that summer's day, all those years ago, when I had that joyous moment of sunlight and freedom as I walked to school from Dad's house. I now get the same feeling of undiluted happiness when I go to my field and breathe the air. I see the sun, I smell the grass, I feel the love there. I breathe in the goodness that I didn't have for so many years. It's been a long, exhausting, sometimes overwhelming struggle to get to this point in my life, but it has been so bloody worth it. The journey to recovery is not over yet, but I will just keep breathing, taking in that lovely fresh air. I just want to keep breathing.

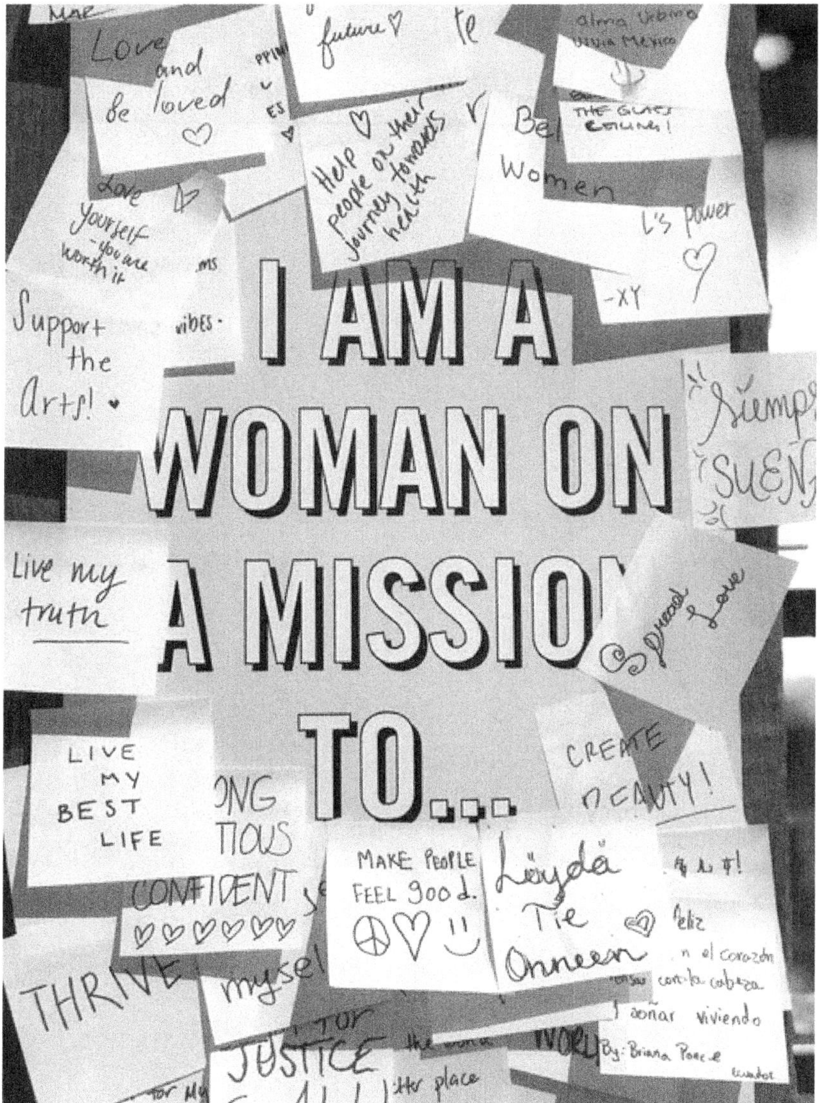
I AM A
WOMAN ON
A MISSIO
TO...
Love and be loved
future
Help people on their journey towards health
Women
Love yourself - you are worth it
Support the Arts!
Live my truth
Spread Love
LIVE MY BEST LIFE
CREATE
CONFIDENT
MAKE PEOPLE FEEL good.
THRIVE
JUSTICE

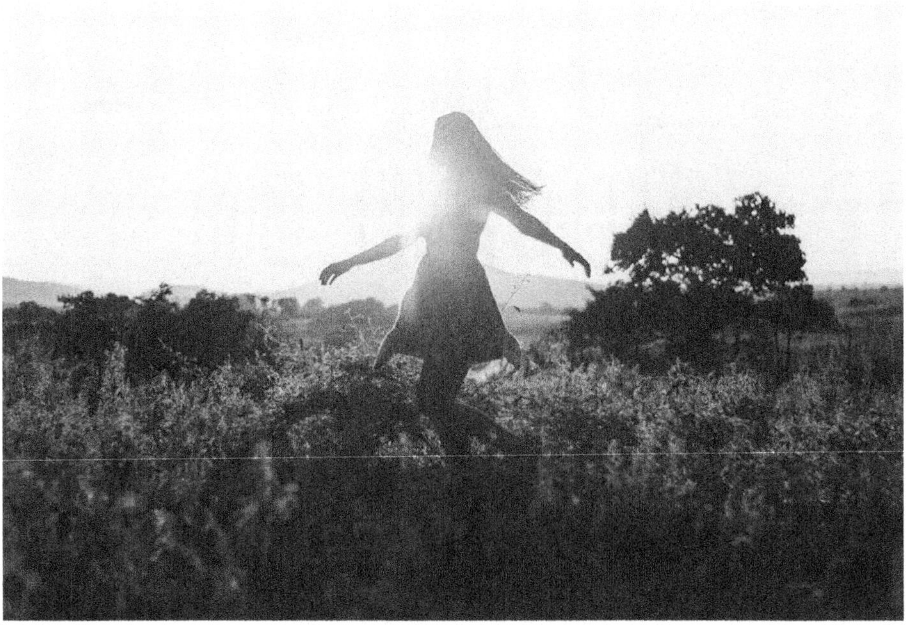

THANK YOU

Derek

I dedicate this book to the one man who held me, lifted me, heard me and loved me. Without his compassion and tenderness, I would be lost in old dark places with a bleak future, or possibly dead. I would have continued my internal belief that I was filth, with no value, and acted as such. This man held my tears and when they poured, his warm, safe arms surrounded me. No advice, no helpful tips, no conversations of what, why, or how, he did not need to. He has loved me in my sorrow and happiness and never tried to speed up my recovery or assume where or how I should be. Derek just allowed me to be me and was always there, even when I could not see or hear the world outside. The courage and resilience I have needed during the slow process of recovery came from Derek's courage and resilience to stand alongside me in all weathers. Recovery depends upon your ability to be vulnerable in a relationship, whether with your partner, friend or therapist. Derek has enabled me to be vulnerable but safe. We laugh together to think how I have transformed into a very different wife, a transformation he has watched over and supported every step of the way. He is the essence of beauty, connection and love. I owe him my life, I really mean this! I know I am a good partner and have shared such a great marriage, but he is the copious carpet of velvet I fell on from the first day I met him. I love you doesn't even touch the sides. x

All of You

I have had many more good people in my life than bad and far too many wonderful people to mention in this small book. Family, friends, instructors, colleagues, drunk or high people, passionate warriors, people I have worked with, trained, yes all of you. Close to my heart are the many, many victims of abuse and violence, both women and girls, who I have been totally blessed to work with. To all the people who have shared books, quotes, poems, podcasts, seminars: you have helped bring life to these disturbing, sensitive topics, truly helping my understanding and making it something I could finally heal from. Thank you all for each experience. To the three wise, wonderful women who have heard parts of my story and counselled me through the last decades, my therapists Anne and Sarah and my clinical supervisor Shirani. You are all collectively part of my story. You have taught me to live, to strive, to challenge, to be courageous, to sing, to love, to get angry and, at last, to find my voice.

I hope this book will encourage others to believe and find their own voice.

My Writer

To the wonderful writer Aileen O'Brien, who has been sensitive, patient and encouraging throughout and whose skills helped tease out this truthful but complex account.

Music

To all those involved in its creation, I say Thank You for the Music. I sang these Abba lyrics as a traumatised child when I would escape from a frightening world into a fantasy where my mother praised my singing and life was joyful. Music has literally kept me alive, easing the pain in my head and body and throughout my life it has been my safest form of soothing and healing. When I look back at where I have come from up until this point, there are four songs that represent my life. 'Grey Day' by Madness represents my childhood; 'Hand in my Pocket' by Alanis Morissette is me ploughing through my adult life, with drink and resilience; 'Dog Days Are Over' by Florence and the Machine is letting go; 'Landslide' by Fleetwood Mac is all about walking forward into peace.

WE HAVE A VOICE

My Sons

Without you both, I am not sure I could have pushed through this far. I want you to know that I have loved you throughout this journey and I want this book to enable you to love, connect and grow as men and support each other with honesty and compassion. I also hope that if there are unanswered questions or feelings you need to process, this is normal and I am here to listen. You are already the men I hoped you would grow to be. My aim was to provide clarity and understanding about who I am and to make sense of feelings that you may not have placed as you were growing up. There may be fears and thoughts I may have unknowingly projected onto you. I have been a mum who has concealed some of my illness and trauma through fear of disturbing you both, but I have grown to realise I never had the control of my mental health in my hands. I started this book at a time when my anxiety was at its worst. I feared I would not have the strength to live through my trauma and believed I may become another suicide statistic, leaving you both to wonder or fantasise the reasons. This was during some of the most harrowing times in my trauma recovery when I was often regressing into the abused, fearful, helpless child. My sons, as you now know, my story has not ended and I plan to live the rest of my life singing, laughing, being annoying and being your mum. I believe I have totally survived the worst and am ready to move on. I spent my life on my story and would like for you both not to get lost in mine but be in your own story, living and loving. Me and dad are your fans forever lol. Mum x

The very last song in this book is for my sons: 'How Long Will I Love You' by Ellie Goulding.

Story Terrace

Printed in Great Britain
by Amazon